*October 4, 1996*

# The Lord Told Me ...
# I Think

## Don Matzat

HARVEST HOUSE PUBLISHERS
Eugene, Oregon 97402

**THE LORD TOLD ME . . . I THINK**

Copyright © 1996 by Harvest House Publishers
Eugene, Oregon 97402

**Library of Congress Cataloging-in-Publication Data**
Matzat, Don.
    The Lord told me —I think / Don Matzat.
        p. cm.
    1. Holy Spirit.   2. Holy Spirit—Biblical teaching.   I. Title.
ISBN 1-56507-370-3
BT121.2.M35   1995
231.7—dc20                                                    95-34636
                                                                    CIP

**Printed in the United States of America.**
96 97 98 99 00 01 02 BC 10 9 8 7 6 5 4 3 2 1

Dedicated to the memory of my
mother and grandmother, who taught
me that believing in Jesus was not only
a matter of the head, but also a
matter of the heart.

# Contents

**6** Contents

# Introduction

God intends for us to live in relationship with him. We were never meant to be independent. I once heard it said that the result of the Adam's rebellion was that Adam and his descendants changed from being dependent upon God to being independent. In other words, by nature we seek to do our own thing. In the life of a Christian, the purpose of sanctification, which means "being set apart for God," is to move us from independence into a greater and greater dependence upon God. I think this is a good definition of the sanctification process.

Even though as fallen humanity we pursue independence, it is never actually achieved. We never live in a vacuum nor really do our own thing. How we live, the decisions we make, the goals we set, and the lifestyle we pursue is established, influenced, led or guided by other outside forces. Each person's decision-making process is able to be labeled. Lifestyle or a worldview is readily identifiable. For example:

If we seek to do our own thing and allow others the same right to do their own thing without any regard for established principles and values, we are *relativists*. This is the prevailing attitude of this so-called post-modern age.

If the decisions we make are governed by what we can obtain such as wealth or material goods, we are *materialists*. Most of us, to one degree or another, are materialists. We are too often led by material pursuits.

If we are practical people and pursue what will produce the greatest results, again with no regard for what might be defined as right or wrong, we are *pragmatists*. And if our decisions vary based upon the circumstances, we are *situationalists*.

If we make decisions that will be of the most benefit to us, believing that we are the measure of all things, we are *humanists*. If we make those decisions with a singular concern for self without any regard for other human beings, we become *objectivists*.

If our life decisions are made with a view to pleasure and our motto is, "If it feels good, do it," we are *hedonists*.

If we believe that our life decisions are previously established by some higher order or wisdom and we seek our destiny in the stars, we are *determinists*.

If we look for outside help and seek wisdom from the spirit world or go after a personal spirit-guide, we are *spiritists* or *occultists*.

If we live by laws, standards of right and wrongs, and value systems and believe that everyone else should do the same, we are *moralists* or *legalists*.

All of these definitions can be put together in varying combinations. A person might be a materialistic humanist, or a relativistic hedonist, and so forth. Of course, if you add to these definitions such mindsets as *conservative* or *liberal* you can really stir up the pot.

What I am trying to say is simple: We are all guided by something or someone outside of us. There is a motivation behind our decisions and pursuits. It may be an ethical system, a mindset, a worldview, a set of values taught by others, or the prevailing philosophy of the age. For example, if you get a divorce because another man or woman gives you more pleasure, your decisions was based on the pursuit of pleasure. You're a hedonist. If you decide to uproot your family and move to a different city because a new job offers more money, you're a materialist. If you decide to get an abortion because having a baby will inconvenience you, you're an objectivist. If you are pro-choice on the abortion issue even though you personally feel that abortion is wrong, you're a relativist. If you believe based upon the absolute moral law that abortion is wrong for everyone, you're a moralist or legalist.

Perhaps the meaning of the tree of the knowledge of good and evil from which Adam and Eve partook in rebellion against God is that all of humanity would be in bondage to some specific system whereby the good and the evil would be defined. Or, as the Bible, says, we became subject to and in bondage to the Law.

Yet, there was one person who walked upon this earth whose lifestyle totally defied definition. That was Jesus Christ. When you read his words or assess his actions as revealed in the four Gospels, you are amazed. What are we to do with him? Was he a legalist, a moralist, a materialist, a relativist? Was Jesus a liberal or a conservative? Try as we might, we are unable to pigeonhole him, because his decisions were led by the Holy Spirit. His will was to do the will of God. He was not living by laws, systems, philosophies, or the prevailing mindset of the age. He was living, acting, moving, and deciding on the basis of his relationship with his Father in heaven. He said, "By myself I can do nothing; I judge only as I hear, and my judgment is just, for I seek not to please myself but him who sent me" (John 5:30).

When you move into the book of Acts, you discover the same dynamic in the early Christians. They were being led by the Spirit, but there was a profound difference between their experience and the experience of Jesus. While Jesus had a human nature, he was without sin. Such was not the case with the early Christians. For this reason, their ability to discern the leading of the Spirit was imperfect. You read about Christian widows from different cultures arguing over food distribution. You encounter church members who lie, Jewish believers who are tradition-minded, apostles who argue, and church conventions called for the purpose of solving disputes.

Yet, the ideal remained. The dynamic of being led by the Spirit was a part of their Christian expectation and experience. The men who were chosen to oversee the food distribution program so that the widows would stop arguing were to be men filled with the Spirit (Acts 6:3). Why? Undoubtedly so that they would exhibit Spirit-led wisdom in their decision making. When the apostles stepped out into ministry, they sought to be led by the Spirit, yet Paul and Barnabas still argued over who to take and where to go (Acts 15:36ff). While their knowledge of God's will was imperfect (1 Corinthians 13:12), they didn't give up and merely resort to common sense. They sought to discern that good and gracious will of God for their lives and ministries (Acts 16:10).

As you read the epistles that contain the teachings of the apostles, you discover the command to be led by the Spirit and walk in the Spirit (Romans 8:14; Galatians 5:18). The flesh and the Spirit are clearly distinguished (Galatians 5:16,17). The dynamic of being filled with the Spirit is explained (Ephesians 5:18-21). In order to discern the will of God, the renewal of the mind is encouraged (Romans 12:2). The fruit or results of walking according to the Spirit is presented (Galatians 5:19-23). The dynamic experience of being led by the Spirit, evidenced in the life of Jesus himself, is taught for the profit of all believers.

Everyone is led by something.

Jesus was led by the Holy Spirit.

The apostles and early Christians were led by the Holy Spirit even though their knowledge of God's will was imperfect.

What are *you* led by?

This book is about divine guidance.

In the minds of some people, this subject would be located on the fringe of theological stability since it is perceived as involving spiritual experiences, subjective impressions, and mystical encounters. It is difficult to find a textbook on systematic theology in which the subject of divine guidance is even mentioned.

Yet, in the age in which we are living, no subject is more compelling. Blaine Smith points out that in the minds of most Christians today, guidance is more than a major concern—it is a primary concern.[1] Many people realize that in the midst of the world's ideologies that are presented in politically correct public education, promoted in popular talk media, or depicted on the silver screen, learning to discern the will of God and seeking to be led by the Spirit is a vital consideration for Christians.

I write from a somewhat unique experience. For 15 years, beginning in 1971, I was a part of the charismatic movement. One of my favorite topics was "the leading of the Holy Spirit." In fact, in the early 1980s, I had an article published in *Charisma* magazine on the subject of guidance titled, "The Lord told me to write this article . . . I think!"

Since 1986, after leaving the charismatic movement, I have settled into being part of a mainline, conservative, theologically solid denomination. While I do not regret leaving the charismatic movement, I do miss the dynamic that is a part of the movement. Charismatic Christians live in the expectation of God acting in the midst of his people. While the movement may have produced some distorted teachings, it has not been guilty of fostering the notion that we should do our own thing or resort to human common sense.

In the pages that follow, I will be sharing with you what I always taught as a pastor in the charismatic movement concerning the subject of guidance or the leading of the Holy Spirit. Nothing has changed except for one thing: *I write this material with great caution.* I know the problems that arise when spiritual experience is emphasized. Inevitably, some people begin to base the certainty of their entire relationship with God on their feelings and experience.

For this reason, before delving into the subject of divine guidance, I will be attempting to help you understand the importance of making a clear distinction between biblical doctrine and subjective experience. Once we set that into place, let's examine together what the Bible has to say about being led by the Holy Spirit.

This is not a book offering engraved-in-stone theological propositions. I am wrestling with what I believe is a very important subject for the people of God. There is much confusion over the issue of guidance. Some Christians have been quick to embrace every voice as being the Holy Spirit, while others have been quick to dismiss any voice as being the Holy Spirit. All I am asking of you, the reader, is to join me in grappling with this issue.

I thank the good folks at Harvest House for their help in presenting this book to you. May God bless you as you read and study.

Donald Matzat
St. Louis, Missouri
July 1, 1995

The Bible speaks of numerous means provided

by God for his people to discover his will.

The singular New Testament means is to

be led by the Holy Spirit.

# I

# "Lord, What Is Your Will for My Life?"

How many times have you asked that question? We all face decisions, and if we are Christians, we desire to do the will of God.

We ask that question when we wonder about our day-to-day decisions and when we are seeking long-term direction for our lives, and rightly so. The Bible says that God prepares good works for us to walk in (Ephesians 2:10). We all know that we should be serving the Lord. "But Lord," we ask, "what is it you want me to do and how will I know that you want me to do it?"

Many of us also ask questions about the future direction of our fellowships, churches, and ministries. Is this what the Lord wants? Does God have a will for our church or our ministry? If so, what is it and how can we discern it?

The desire to know the will of God is a legitimate Christian concern. M. Blaine Smith writes:

Our concern with knowing the will of God is not hard to understand. It springs from curiosity and a natural need for direction. On the deepest level, it reflects

15

our desire to be accountable to Christ and a profound concern to accomplish something significant with our lives.[1]

Dr. J. I. Packer echoes the same sentiment:

Healthy Christians, however, while valuing advice, look to God also. There are many promises of Divine direction in Scripture, and many testimonies to its reality. It is wrong for Christians not to seek God's help in making the choices, commitments and decisions that shape their lives.[2]

If we as Christians are not concerned with knowing and doing the will of God, then we may need to ask some very serious questions about our faith in Jesus Christ. God paid a great price to buy us back from sin, death, and the power of the devil. The death of Jesus Christ reconciled us with God so that we now have access to him through the ministry of the Holy Spirit. Our relationship with God does not only mean that one day we will live with him in heaven. It also means that we live in constant relationship with him and seek to do his will today. As the apostle Paul stated in Romans 5:1, now that we have been declared right with God, we have peace with God and access to his grace. Are you making the most of that access?

## Thy Word Is a Lamp
## unto My Feet

God has not left us in the dark concerning his will for our lives. He has revealed his will in the Bible. The psalmist describes the Word of God as being a lamp to our feet and a light to our path (Psalm 119:105). The Bible gives us clear direction. Whether or not a person should get a divorce, commit adultery, live a homosexual lifestyle, get an abortion, go out and get drunk, or cheat in business is clearly answered in the Bible. Even in the light of rational argumentation, when it comes to the killing of an abortion doctor, the Bible clearly says, "Don't kill!" (*see* Exodus 20:13). For these kinds of decisions, we do not need to seek the will of God.

The Bible provides an abundance of clear direction for our Christian lives. Should we join a Christian congregation, get involved in the study of God's Word, worship the Lord regularly, support the work of the kingdom with our finances, use our gifts and abilities for God's glory, and forgive people who have wronged us? Those are not debatable issues. God's will concerning those matters is clearly revealed in Scripture.

## How and When

Sometimes the Bible does not tell us everything we want to know. While there are general *what* directions, the specific *how* and *when* are not spelled out.

"Lord," you might ask, "I know that it is your will for me to share my faith with others, but to whom do you want me to witness and when?" Or, "I know, Father, that you want me to use my gifts to serve you, but how should I go about doing that?"

The issue of *how* and *when* is very important. For example, I believe Abraham sincerely attempted to do God's will when he decided to begin the great nation of Israel by taking his wife's maidservant, Hagar, and producing Ishmael (Genesis 16). For Abraham to have a son was *what* God wanted. But it certainly was not done *how* or *when* he wanted it. Abraham's union with Hagar began the Islamic nation. Thus, his jump ahead of God had disastrous results.

Many years ago when I was about 10 years old I decided to surprise my father and do what he wanted done. It was Christmastime, and I knew that my father wanted the Christmas tree set up and decorated. One Saturday morning while the rest of the family was out shopping, I went into the garage, dragged the Christmas tree into the living room, put it in the stand, strung on the lights, hung the ornaments, and tossed on the icicles. Then I stepped back to admire my handiwork. In my childish eyes, it looked pretty good.

Well, when my dad got home, he was furious. I did *what* he wanted done, but I didn't do it *how* or *when* he wanted it done. Now he was faced with the task of taking everything apart and doing it over again.

I have been involved in numerous attempts to develop God-pleasing ministries. There have been situations in which we have had to take things apart and do them over again. Could the reason be that we failed to seek the Lord for the how and when? I believe so!

## When Scripture Is Silent

What should we do when the Bible is silent concerning the how and when? Are we on our own? Is the decision up to us to do whatever we think is right or pleases us?

According to the Bible, the answer is no. For example, read what James has to say:

> Now listen, you who say, "Today or tomorrow we will go to this or that city, spend a year there, carry on business and make money." Why, you do not even know what will happen tomorrow. What is your life? You are a mist that appears for a little while and then vanishes. Instead, you ought to say, "If it is the Lord's will we will live and do this or that" (James 4:13-15).

How do we know what is the Lord's will and whether or not we should go into the city and buy and sell? Is James telling us that we should simply say, "If it is God's will" and wait to see what happens? Or is he also encouraging us to *seek and discern* God's will? James clearly tells us in his epistle that if we lack wisdom, we should ask the Lord for it (James 1:5).

The leaders of the nation of Israel were expected to seek the Lord for wisdom and guidance prior to making decisions. For example, the men of Israel entered into a covenant with the Gibeonites, who tricked the Israelites into believing that they came from a faraway country and were not among the peoples who were to be defeated and removed from the land. Why were the Israelite leaders tricked? We read in Joshua 9:14 that the men of Israel *did not ask direction from the Lord.*

At the end of the book of Judges (21:25), the nation of Israel is described as being without a king. Therefore, "everyone did as he saw fit." People did what was right in their own eyes.

Could it be that some of our plans have gone awry, wrong decisions have been made, fellowships and ministries have dried up, and ministers have fallen by the wayside because of our failure to seek direction from the Lord? Have we, like the nation of Israel, sometimes succumbed to doing that which is right in our own eyes?

## Seeking the Will of God

In the Old Testament, God provided his people with some interesting means for seeking and determining his will.

First, the priests were in possession of the Urim and Thummim, devices used to receive a yes or no answer to a particular question addressed to God (see, for example, 1 Samuel 23:9-12; 30:7-8).

We do not know what the Urim and Thummim were. We do know that they were kept on the person of the priest. They were probably small items, similar to a pair of dice that were rolled and produced two possible outcomes: yes or no. I guess we could say it would be similar to praying and flipping a coin.

After the time of David, there is no mention of the Urim and Thummim. Some scholars believe that after the rise of the prophets who spoke forth the will of God, the Urim and Thummim were no longer necessary.

In addition to the Urim and Thummim, the "casting of lots" was a popular means for determining the will of God. The land of Israel was apportioned to the tribes of Israel by lot (Joshua 14:2). The lot was cast to determine who was guilty of breaking God's law (Joshua 7:14). On the great Day of Atonement, the goat for sacrifice and the scapegoat were chosen by lot (Leviticus 16:7-10). To this day we do not know exactly how the casting of lots was done; the character and form of the lot in ancient Israel were not preserved or recorded.

The practice of casting of lots continued into the New Testament. The Greek word for *lot* means "inheritance"—what has been assigned to a person by God. The method of casting lots in the New Testament probably involved placing different colored stones into a vessel and shaking the vessel until one stone jumped out. At the cross, the soldiers cast lots for the garments of Jesus.

In the book of Acts, which recounts the development of the Christian church, there is only one incident of casting lots—the selecting of the apostle who would replace Judas. Following the outpouring of the Holy Spirit on the day of Pentecost, the decisions and directions of the church were led by the Holy Spirit.

## Led by the Holy Spirit

While the book of Acts is defined as the "acts of the apostles," it is more correct to say that it chronicles the acts of the Holy Spirit. In the beginning of the book, Luke states that after Jesus ascended into heaven, he continued to lead and guide the church through the Holy Spirit.

We see this illustrated in the story of the Ethiopian in Acts 8. He was rolling along in his chariot reading Isaiah chapter 53. Philip the evangelist happened to be nearby. We read in verse 29, "The Spirit told Philip, 'Go to that chariot and stay near it.'" After Philip shared the good news, the Ethiopian believed and was baptized.

Another major event in Acts was the conversion of the Gentiles. How did that come about? Both Cornelius and Peter had dreams. Men were sent to Peter, and the Spirit told Peter to go with them to the house of Cornelius (Acts 11:12). Peter preached. The Holy Spirit descended, and unbelievers were brought to faith.

We also see that it was the Holy Spirit who sent Saul and Barnabas on a missionary journey (Acts 13:4). And on Paul's second missionary journey, the Spirit hindered the apostles from entering into both Asia and Mysia. We read in Acts 16:6-7:

> Paul and his companions traveled throughout the region of Phrygia and Galatia, having been kept by the Holy Spirit from preaching the word in the province of Asia. When they came to the border of Mysia, they tried to enter Bithynia but the Spirit of Jesus would not allow them to.

In Acts 15, when dealing with the question of what to do with the Gentile converts, the council at Jerusalem reached their decision because "it seemed good to the Holy Spirit and also to us" (verse 28).

How did the Holy Spirit accomplish this work of leading, guiding, and directing the church? How did the Holy Spirit tell Philip to draw near to the chariot of the Ethiopian (Acts 8:29)? How did the Holy Spirit tell Peter to go with the three men to the house of Cornelius (Acts 11:12)? How did the Holy Spirit forbid Paul and the apostolic company from entering Asia and Bithynia (Acts 16:6-7)? What was the dynamic involved?

While the Bible does not specifically answer how the Holy Spirit did his work, we can arrive at deductions. There is no reason to believe that these people experienced an external invasion of the Holy Spirit from without, similar to what happened at the baptism of Jesus when the Holy Spirit appeared in the form of a dove. Based on the teaching of the apostles in their letters to the various churches, the Holy Spirit led them internally—through their thoughts, ideas, and insights. There was something going on within Philip, Peter, and the apostolic company that brought them to conclude that the Holy Spirit was speaking and leading. There was "an inner witness of the Spirit."

Circumstances must have had a role as well. Paul told the Corinthians that he was staying at Ephesus because a door of ministry remained open for him (1 Corinthians 16:9). He asked the Colossians to pray for him so that a door would be opened for his message (Colossians 4:3).

The Holy Spirit also gave direction through the prophetic words of other Christians such as Ananias, who was sent by the Holy Spirit to Saul after his conversion (Acts 9:15-17), and Agabus, who warned Paul about the danger of going to Jerusalem (Acts 21:10-11).

The book of Acts defines numerous instances of the Holy Spirit guiding people through dreams, visions, and the appearance of angels. The recipients of the Spirit's guidance included Ananias and Paul (9:11-5), Peter and Cornelius (10:3-6), the man of Macedonia (16:9), and Philip (Acts 8:26).

The Christian church was not built by human wisdom, insight, and power, but by the Holy Spirit. The early Christians were led by the Spirit, hindered by the Spirit, sent out by the Spirit, and instructed by the Spirit. He opened doors and closed doors. He prepared the good works that these Christians walked in (Ephesians 2:10).

## Is This for Today?

Was the Holy Spirit's leading and guiding in the book of Acts an extraordinary operation that is not available for us today? Did the first-century Christians have the benefit of being led by the Holy Spirit while we are left to do our own thing or formulate our decisions based on inferences from the biblical record or the use of common sense?

In some ways, the apostles did experience an extraordinary working of the Spirit. For example, the books that we write today are not of the same inspired, inerrant nature as the books of the Bible, which were written by the apostles and prophets. Their writings are unique.

In addition, many of the powerful miracles performed by the apostles were extraordinary. Even though God may choose to work similar miracles today, the miracles of the apostles had the unique purpose of confirming their proclamation of the Gospel message (Hebrews 2:3-4). Today, we have this same proclamation in written form—the Bible. If people want to know whether we are speaking the Word of God, they do not look for us to perform miracles. Rather, they simply compare what we preach with the message recorded in the Bible by the miracle-working apostles and prophets.

But what about the *dynamic* of the leading of the Holy Spirit experienced by the apostles? Was *that* unique?

To determine whether various workings of the Holy Spirit were limited to the first-century era or if they have ongoing application for us today, we must look for the commands and promises of Scripture. A careful search reveals that there are no commands and promises in the Bible that say we will write inerrant documents and perform miracles to prove that the Word of God is being spoken. However, there *are* clear commands and promises about being led by the Spirit. Jesus promised that the Holy Spirit would always be present with his people (Matthew 28:20; John 16:5-11). The Bible commands us to be led by the Spirit (Romans 8:14; Galatians 5:18), and teaches us how to be led by him.

While it is true that there was an extraordinary operation of the Holy Spirit in the first century, there is nothing in the Bible to suggest that the *guidance* of the Holy Spirit—especially by way of his inner witness, or his use of circumstances, or the "prophetic" words of one Christian to another—is unique. Perhaps we could speak of dreams, visions, and the appearance of angels as being unique, but I believe that this was also unique for the first-century Christians. But the command and promise to be led by the Holy Spirit still remains with us through today. He desires to lead and guide us as he did the Christians of the first century.

Basing our knowledge of God and his will upon subjective impression easily leads to deception and fraud. In fact, if we base the certainty of our eternal salvation on our feelings, our salvation may be at risk.

# 2

# Hotline to Heaven?

In the church today there is much confusion over the issue of spiritual experience. There are two extremes. Some Bible teachers and pastors give spiritual experience a lot of emphasis in the Christian life. Others find no place for it.

Before we begin discussing the experience of being led by the Holy Spirit, we must take care to define it properly within the context of Christian truth. The subject of spiritual experience is fraught with potential pitfalls, and as responsible Christians, we must take the time to understand what the Bible says about this vital ingredient in the life and piety of the Christian church.

## Teachings Without Biblical Support

For 15 years I was actively involved in and promoted the teachings of the charismatic movement. I truly enjoyed the friendships that I formed with my charismatic brothers and sisters, and I loved the dynamic that was a part of the movement. But in 1986, after much inner turmoil, I renounced my involvement and left the movement. Let me tell you why . . .

As one of the leaders in the Lutheran segment of the renewal, I was embroiled in one controversy after the other over the relationship between biblical truth and spiritual experience. I refused to accept strange teachings and phenomena that had no basis in Scripture. I refused to embrace the controversial discipleship teaching that entered the movement in the seventies. There was no biblical basis for the concept of absolute submission to a pyramid of shepherds. I rejected the spurious experience of being slain in the spirit. When people fell over after I prayed for them, I asked them to get up, and they did. Some thought I was "quenching the Spirit." I could find no biblical warrant for the popular practices of binding demons, healing family trees, or visualizing new waves of the Spirit.

I did a major study that uncovered the Jungian roots of the charismatic inner-healing experience, which led to my first book *Inner Healing: Deliverance or Deception*. As a result, a popular, self-styled, inner-healing charismatic prophet accused me of coming against God's anointed—namely, him. He predicted that the Lord was going to get me and my family. That was the response I got for pointing out that much of what was being taught by charismatics was not supported in God's Word.

## The Authority of the Scripture

It was not possible for me to be a part of the charismatic movement and still adhere to the singular authority of the Word of God, the Bible. I was not willing to yield the truth of "Scripture alone" in order to embrace strange spiritual experiences and distorted teachings.

My commitment to Scripture was not motivated by a conservative, fundamentalist mentality, but by the fear of leading people astray. The Bible tell us clearly that teachers of the Word will be judged on a higher standard (James 3:1), and the thought of having a millstone around my neck and being tossed into the sea was not pleasant (*see* Matthew 18:6).

Some years earlier a relative and his family joined a charismatic church that adopted some very bizarre teachings. They were taught to embrace the culture of Judaism. I saw firsthand the danger of leading people beyond the parameters of God's Word. Eventually the leader of the group was exposed as a fraud. My relative and his entire family had been deceived, and it took them years to recover. Upon seeing their pain and confusion, I made a commitment not to go beyond biblical truth into questionable teachings and experiences.

I do not regret my decision to leave the charismatic movement. Shortly after doing so, all the hoopla surrounding the charismatic televangelists broke out. I was glad that I wouldn't be tainted by that via "guilt by association." And today in the mid-nineties, I am happy I'm not in the middle of the controversies generated by the worldwide "Holy Laughter" movement or the questionable "Toronto Blessing." I feel sorry for responsible charismatic leaders like *Charisma* magazine editor Steve Strang who, on the one hand, would like to be in the flow of these "revivals," but on the other hand, feels that all experience must have a basis in Scripture.[1] He seems to be stuck between a rock and a hard place.

## "The Lord Told Me..."

What disturbed me the most about some charismatic teachers was their almost flippant attitude about hearing special messages from God. They often gave the impression that they had a hotline to heaven and that God had nothing better to do than talk with them. They punctuated their teaching and preaching with "the Lord told me," "the Lord impressed upon me," "the Lord showed me," or "the Lord laid on my heart."

Why is this type of rhetoric so rampant among charismatics?

A great deal of charismatic teaching, since it deals with experience, is based upon private interpretation, speculation, and opinion. While the charismatic experiences of speaking in tongues, interpretation of tongues, prophecy, and healing do have a precedent in Scripture, the question of *how* those experiences might be manifested today is not clearly revealed in Scripture. In order to teach and write on those subjects, conjecture is required.

If you believe, as charismatics teachers and authors do, that the movement to restore these experiences is a divinely ordained visitation of the Spirit, you would not teach on a given topic and say, "This is what I think . . ." or, "This is how I interpret. . . . " Rather, you would say, "This is what the Lord told me . . ." or "This is what the Lord showed me about that verse. . . ."

I do not question the sincerity of those who claim "the Lord told me . . ." if that is what they believe to be true. Maybe they are right, and perhaps the Lord did tell them. The problem is, when a charismatic teacher equates what he believes "the Lord told him" with what the Lord told the apostles and prophets, the potential for fraud, deception, and false teaching is readily created.

## Fraud

It is easy to manipulate people with the claim that a certain message came from the Lord. Pastors of charismatic fellowships or charismatic televangelists may attempt to move their constituency to financially support a specific work by appealing to what they claim the Lord wants. The issue is not, "Please support my ministry," but rather, "Obey the Holy Spirit; this is what the Lord told me."

Many of the people who comprise charismatic fellowships are easily swayed by what they hear. Coming out of denominations where perhaps the church and ministry were operated as a secular business with the pastor being more of a CEO than a spiritual shepherd, they long to be led by the Spirit. They gravitate to pastors who claim to have a hotline to heaven rather than just a good education.

Some years ago my wife and I attended the Sunday evening worship service of a large charismatic fellowship in Orange County, California. When it came time to take the offering, the head pastor stood up and made a proper financial appeal, but he didn't stop there.

"This is what we are going to do," he went on. "We are going to ask the Looord," his voice quivering, "to take up this offering for us. We are going to pray that the Holy Spirit determines what you should give to support his work."

"And now," he continued, gathering emotional momentum, "I want all eyes closed and every head bowed, and we pray, 'Holy Spirit of God, put into the minds of these, your faithful people, what you would have them to give to support this mighty work. In Jeeesus' name. Amen and Amen!'"

After the prayer ended, he asked us to keep our eyes closed and our heads bowed. He continued in a quiet, gentle manner, "Whatever amount of money pops into your mind, this is what the Holy Spirit wants you to give. It is my duty as God's called and anointed servant to remind you of the importance of obeying God. When you hear the voice of the Lord, do not harden your heart, but obey! Ushers, please come forward. . . ."

Well, needless to say, a dollar amount popped into my mind. Since this was allegedly the Holy Spirit talking to me—the same Holy Spirit who participated in the creation of the heavens and the earth—the figure was not 50 cents. It was a rather sizable amount. In fact, it was just about everything I had in my wallet. And, because I was gullible, I gave it.

Some years later I was a part of a committee that set up a large charismatic conference. The budget for the conference was large. By the time the last night rolled around, the money we had raised still fell short of covering our budget. So we asked one of the Pentecostal pastors who had been on the program to "take the offering." And he did, using the same technique that I described earlier. We raised about $35,000 that night and exceeded our budget. But does the end justify the means?

In my opinion, there would have been no problem if the pastor who took the offering had said,

"If you have a thought in your mind as to how much you should give, it *may* be the Holy Spirit. *You discern it.* If you believe it is the Holy Spirit, then obey what you think is the voice of the Lord."

That is proper. There is nothing wrong with it.

But to say, "The thought is from the Holy Spirit, and *you had better obey it*" could be nothing less than spiritual fraud.

## Deception

It's not too difficult for us to discern that many of the spiritual experiences claimed by charismatic figures are deceptive.

For example, popular "faith teacher" Kenneth Hagin claims that Jesus came into his room one day, sat down by his bedside, and talked with him for about 30 minutes. During that time, Jesus allegedly taught him how to be led by the inner witness of the Holy Spirit. And that's not the only visit; Hagin claims that Jesus has appeared to him eight times—seven times barefoot, and one time wearing Roman sandals. Hagin describes Jesus as 5 feet and 11 inches tall and weighing about 180 pounds.[2]

Kenneth Hagin's claims simply are not possible. In 2 Corinthians 5:16, the apostle Paul makes it clear that we no longer regard Jesus Christ according to the flesh. If the resurrected, ascended, glorified Christ, who is truly God, chose to visit the bedside of Kenneth Hagin for a midnight chat, then he would not be wearing sandals, and Hagin would be toast.

I don't know what Hagin's motives are for making these claims. He seems to be trying to make people believe that his teachings have the same authority as what the Bible teaches. Perhaps he firmly believes that it is the will of God for people to embrace what he teaches and, in his mind, whatever means are used to accomplish that end—even if it means claiming that he gets his teaching directly from Jesus—are justified.

This way of thinking seems to exist among some charismatic teachers. For example, after it was revealed that Evangelist Peter Popoff's words of knowledge were electronically produced, he responded by saying, "All I am trying to do is build up the faith of people."

Many years ago I started writing a manuscript of my testimony for a small charismatic publisher. Since my testimony was not all that exciting, I was encouraged to enlarge upon it and make up extravagant stories about the power of the Holy Spirit. The publisher explained, "We want people to believe the message of the book. If you can accomplish that by making up stories, then I believe God will be pleased." I refused.

Now I do believe that the message of *this* book is timely for people today. And I suppose that if I were to say that Jesus himself revealed the contents of this book to me and if I made up a story of how that revelation took place, perhaps more people would read the book and learn to trust the leading of the Holy Spirit. The question is, does the end justify the means? I think not! For me to make such a claim would be deceptive. It would be on par with what Joseph Smith did—he started a new religion by claiming to find golden tablets, and "translating" what is now known as the Book of Mormon, which he said was buried in a mountain in upstate New York.

## False Teaching

There are charismatics today who claim that the Holy Spirit is bringing great revival to the church through a worldwide phenomenon called "Holy Laughter"—a movement whose main figure is South African Rodney Howard-Browne. A sister revival, known as the "Toronto Blessing," began in 1994 at the Airport Vineyard in Toronto. That church is now visited by thousands of people each week who want to experience "carpet time" or witness the hysterical behavior that is manifest when a person is allegedly touched by the Spirit.

I do not believe the Holy Spirit is producing the belly laughs or the strange experiences associated with these phenomena, nor am I willing to say that he might be. First of all, what we see happening in this movement is contrary to what 1 Corinthians 14 says about frenzied, chaotic behavior. Second, the dynamic is readily understood psychologically.

If, for example, David Letterman of late-night TV fame was in the same kind of "authority" position, using the same rhetoric and methodology, he would be more effective in getting belly laughs from the congregation because he is a better comedian. Third, on the day of Pentecost, *everyone* in the Upper Room was touched by the Spirit. But in the Howard-Browne fiasco, only those in the auditorium who are willing to "move with God" are touched. Fourth, if the power and holiness of God were to fill a room, nobody would be laughing. And finally, the Holy Spirit proceeds from the Father and the Son using the vehicle of the Word. He is not dispensed by Howard-Browne or any other human vessel.

## Am I a Skeptic?

Perhaps some of you are asking, "How do you know that it isn't the Holy Spirit putting certain thoughts into the minds of people? How do you know that it isn't the Holy Spirit revealing to charismatic teachers the nature of speaking in tongues? How do you know that Jesus did not appear to Kenneth Hagin? How do you know that Rodney Howard-Browne isn't the greatest revivalist since the apostle Paul?"

When I mentioned these concerns one afternoon on my daily radio talk show, one charismatic listener called in to voice her objection to what I was saying. "Why are you always so skeptical?" she asked angrily. "How do you know their claims are not true?"

Her question, however, is not what we as Christians need to ask. The burden of disproof is not mine or ours. People can make any claim they want—from UFO alien abduction to Betty Eadie's incredible NDE (near-death experience) event. If you question the claims, the supporters can readily respond, "How do you know it isn't true?" But that is not the point.

In all of these matters, the issue is not, How do I know it is not the Holy Spirit? Rather, the issue is, How did that pastor in Orange County *know* it was the Holy Spirit telling people how much they should give to his ministry? How do charismatic teachers *know* that the Lord is speaking to them? How do they *know* that the Holy Spirit is reviving the church by causing people to laugh?

## The Heart of Theology

The answer to those questions is very important because it gets right to the heart of the problem in much of the charismatic teaching we hear and read today. In the study of philosophy, this issue is defined as the epistemological question: *How do you know?*

At the time of the Reformation, when people spoke out in opposition to the Roman Catholic Church's understanding of authority, the truth of *Sola Scriptura* or "Scripture alone" emerged. These people realized that the Bible was the sole source and norm for all truth pertaining to the Christian faith. In answer to the question, "How do you know?" the Reformers replied, "Because Scripture says so!"

The Reformers realized the grave danger of basing faith upon experience. They focused upon the great objective acts of God in Christ Jesus. They taught people to know that their sins were forgiven, that they had the righteousness of Christ, and that they were going to heaven *because the Bible said so*. Faith that is based on experience provides no certainty because experiences are constantly changing and are interpreted by the fallible perceptions of man, whose heart is deceitful (Jeremiah

17:9). When we trust experiences to validate our salvation, our eternal destiny could very well be in jeopardy. The confirmation that we are saved must come from scriptural truth alone.

It is interesting to note that this issue creates no problem for charismatic Roman Catholics. They appeal to the authority of the Church rather than to the authority of Scripture. For example, Fr. Robert DeGrandis, in his booklet *The Gift of Tongues,* answers the question, "How do you know that you are speaking in tongues?" by saying, "The Church indicates that praying in tongues is truly of the Spirit. . . . If praying in tongues is not of the Holy Spirit . . . then the Church has led us down a primrose path."[3]

The question, then, becomes this: If charismatic *Roman Catholics* are wrong because the Church has led them down the primrose path, who is responsible for leading *non-Catholic* charismatics down the primrose path? The answer is simple: Charismatic personalities, leaders, pastors, and self-appointed prophets.

## "Good Morning, Holy Spirit"

One of the best-selling books of the past few years is *Good Morning, Holy Spirit,* written by Pentecostal pastor and televangelist Benny Hinn. While this book includes some legitimate observations about the dynamic working of the Holy Spirit—a dynamic that is often missing in churches that emphasize doctrine—it also contains material that is confusing and potentially harmful. For example, when he discusses the question of Christian knowledge, Hinn writes:

> Let me ask another question. Do you know that you have been saved from sin? Well, how do you know it?

Did you hear a celestial voice from heaven? Did Jesus appear in a physical body and say, "You are saved"?

Someone recently asked me, "Benny, how do you know you are saved?" All I could say was, "I know that I know, that I know, that I know, that I know." That's the strength, the assurance, the Holy Spirit has given to me.

During a church building program, I was asked, "How do you know you're doing the right thing?" *The answer was the same as if I'd been asked about my salvation. "I know that I know, that I know."* The Lord, through the Holy Spirit, told me to start building. Every decision in my life is based on that same inner voice (emphasis added).[4]

That is very dangerous teaching! Contrary to what Benny Hinn thinks, his salvation, the forgiveness of his sins, and his eternal life in heaven is based upon the sure Word of God, not some inner experience. The Bible says that Jesus Christ took upon himself the sins of mankind, died on the cross, and rose again on the third day. Because of this, Benny Hinn is forgiven and saved. The Holy Spirit gave saving faith to Hinn when Hinn received the Gospel message of Jesus Christ.

What if Benny Hinn's "inner witness" to build a church was merely his own imagination and his building program went "belly up"? Would his assurance of salvation also go "belly up"? If the two are based on the same inner voice, and one is wrong, the other would also be wrong.

## Is It the Holy Spirit?

I believe in spiritual experiences. I believe that the Holy Spirit can lead us in our decision-making. I believe that the Spirit dwells within us and can lead us through our thoughts, insights, and ideas. After all, if the devil, the world, and our sinful nature can work within us, we would be foolish to deny that same power to the Holy Spirit. I believe there is an inner witness of the Spirit.

But I also believe that spiritual experiences must be placed into the proper theological contexts so that we can avoid fraud, deception, and false teaching.

Christians who are a part of mainline denominations often give the impression that there is no place in Christian truth for spiritual experience or personal piety. The biblical record and the testimony of other Christians demonstrate otherwise.

# 3

# The Other Side
# of the Coin

One evening after a Bible class, I heard one woman say to another, "When I experienced the inner witness of the Spirit in my heart, I knew Jesus was Lord."

I could not leave such a statement unchallenged. I jumped into the conversation and said, "That's not true!"

She looked at me as if to say, "Who do you think you are telling me what is true and not true?"

"Of course it is true," she replied. "When the Holy Spirit filled my heart, he gave me the inner witness that Jesus truly is my Lord."

"No," I said. "You know Jesus is Lord because the Bible says he is Lord. The Holy Spirit simply opened your eyes to the truth of Scripture and witnessed to your heart that Jesus is Lord."

"Well, yes . . ." she replied somewhat hesitantly. "But I do know that Jesus Christ is Lord!"

Many pastors who are sensitive to doctrine get nervous when they encounter Christians who base their beliefs on their inner experiences—and it's not because they are stuck-in-the-mud traditionalists. They are

concerned about the eternal salvation of their people,
which should be a pastor's primary interest. They are
afraid that if a person is convinced of his salvation and
forgiveness on the basis of an *experience*, then that person
will doubt his salvation and forgiveness should the experience ever be called into question. As you can see, then,
it is dangerous to base your beliefs upon your experience.

There is no doubt that one of the tasks of the Holy
Spirit is to graciously open our eyes to the truth of
Scripture and to witness or confirm that truth to our
hearts, but our knowledge of that truth is based upon
Scripture, not our experience. *The Holy Spirit is our
teacher, but the Bible is his only textbook.*

## Irreconcilable Differences?

I have met many pastors and theologians who want nothing to do with spiritual experience or feelings. They see
those as threats to their theological perspectives. When it
comes to the subject of guidance, rather than relying
upon "subjective speculation," they often resort to what
becomes unaided reason or common sense. They may
open their church or ministry meetings with prayer and
devotions, but they often make decisions in the same
manner any secular corporate Board of Directors would
make decisions—they rely on their own wisdom and not
the Spirit's guidance. They leave the impression that
"God helps those who help themselves."

In today's church, solid biblical theology and spiritual
experience (such as being led by the Holy Spirit) are often
viewed as mutually exclusive. Churches with a solid biblical
theology frequently place little emphasis on spiritual
experience. In fact, some churches even will downgrade it.

And churches that emphasize spiritual experience often lack solid theology, and perhaps even scoff at those who have a high regard for theology.

Some years ago I was discussing this seemingly irreconcilable problem with a charismatic evangelist.

"You know, Jim," I said. "I get so tired of charismatic chaos. I long to get back into the solid doctrinal security of my denomination."

"Brother Don," he replied, somewhat disturbed. "You will find that there is no chaos in a cemetery."

While I believe his cemetery metaphor was grossly overstated, in his mind there were only two options: *spiritual death* or *spiritual chaos*. But was he right? If so, why or why not? God is neither the source of spiritual death nor the author of spiritual confusion.

I recently received a letter from a listener of my daily radio talk show. She asked, "Can you recommend a church that teaches solid theology and the experience of the Holy Spirit?"

I wrote her and answered, "I'm sorry, but I cannot help you."

While churches that offer that combination may exist, I did not know of any.

If the church of Jesus Christ is going to be what God intends for it to be, sound doctrine and spiritual experience, the mind and the heart, must find a way to come together. Mike Horton is correct when he says,

> The divorce between doctrine and piety, the mind and the heart, characteristic of both orthodox Reformation folk today on one side and pietists and charismatics on the other, is a course for disaster, not for either reformation or revival.[1]

## Stop Scoffing!

One of my heroines is my little Lithuanian grandmother. It seemed to me that she had discovered a correct balance between biblical understanding and heartfelt experience. Just about every time we went to visit her in her farm-house in Connecticut, she was seated in the dining room reading her Lithuanian Bible. She had committed large portions of Scripture to memory.

She also had a "heart for Jesus." She loved the popular gospel song "In the Garden." Since she loved to work in her garden, the thought of Jesus walking and talking with her was very precious. And, you know, I think he did walk and talk with her!

After spending a few years in seminary, I accepted the opinion of one deep-thinking, objective-minded professor who made the statement in class that "In the Garden" was probably the worst hymn ever written because it focused upon personal feelings and experience rather than the great historical truths of Scripture.

One day I mentioned to my mother that I felt that grandma's favorite hymn was one of the worst ever written. Normally, my mom would not lose her cool, but this time she got rather angry with me. She scowled and said, "Donald, who do you think you are criticizing the faith of my mother? She probably knows more about what it means to be a Christian than you will ever know!"

I have come to believe that some of the theologians and doctrinal clergy who are so quick to scoff at the heart-felt spirituality of other Christians should heed the same rebuke. Perhaps they make light of spiritual experience because of their own lack of the same. I knew one theologian who explained his ever-increasing baldness by saying that the Holy Spirit was continually hitting him on the top of the head trying to get his theology into his heart. Perhaps we need more bald theologians?

## Back to the Reformation

There is a positive, growing movement today that is calling the church back to the principles of the Reformation. Responding to the bad theology or even lack of theology that often exists among charismatics and evangelicals, men like Michael Horton, R.C. Sproul, Robert Preus, J. I. Packer, and John Armstrong, being a part of both Calvinist and Lutheran traditions, are spearheading a movement that calls the church back to the basic objective biblical truths observed by reformers in the sixteenth and seventeenth centuries, especially the cardinal doctrine of justification by grace through faith.

I count myself as a part of that movement. I strongly believe that an emphasis upon solid biblical theology is sorely needed today to bring balance to the confusing evangelical and charismatic emphasis upon experience. Such emphasis leads to dangerous and distorted claims and teachings. If, for example, charismatic teachers believed the reformers' observation that the Word of God is the vehicle through which the Holy Spirit operates, they would not embrace Rodney Howard-Browne as a "dispenser of the Holy Ghost."

There are some responsible leaders in the charismatic movement who recognize this very need. For example, Jack Hayford, pastor of Church on the Way in Van Nuys, California, says,

> First, we must avoid the arrogance that supposes theology is arthritic or that history is a waste of time. We must take time to investigate the church's history.

We must bother to examine the theological implications of our experiences. If our experiences truly ver-
ify the Word, they'll fit into sound theology.
Remember, vital revivalists and reformers of church
history—such as Luther, Wesley and Finney—were
not theological wimps. Both distant and recent
church history remind us of the folly of free-wheeling
revelation without foundation.[2]

If this movement is going to succeed in calling the
church back to good theology, the orthodox, Reformation-
type Christians must find a place for spiritual experience
and the feelings of the heart. Some of them have a hard
time fitting it in. Once when I talked about the leading of
the Holy Spirit in our decision-making, a Reformed theologian said he believed that because he was a Christian,
*everything* he did was led by the Spirit.

Yet that kind of thinking did not characterize the great
reformers Martin Luther and John Calvin. In his 1535
commentary on the book of Galatians, Martin Luther
paraphrases the words of the apostle Paul in Galatians 5:16
by saying:

For the Spirit struggles against the flesh and the flesh
against the Spirit. All I am requiring of you now—and
for that matter, all you are able to produce—is that
you follow the guidance of the Spirit and resist the
guidance of the flesh.[3]

And John Calvin, a strong proponent of rational faith,
did not want to return to Geneva to lead the Reformation
in that city but he did because he felt the Holy Spirit
nudging him in that direction.

Perhaps the people who choose to reject the guidance
of the Holy Spirit should at least reinstate the Urim and
Thummim or the casting of lots. That would at least

counter the impression that Christians are called to do what is right in their own eyes. There has never been a time when God did not provide some means or method for his followers to seek and discern his will.

On the positive side, Christians who embrace the biblical understanding that emerged out of the sixteenth-century Reformation are not easily led astray. They are committed to their doctrines and traditions and not readily pulled into cults, heresies, or errors. If a person knocked on their door and declared, "The Lord told me to tell you to support my ministry," they would laugh and politely shut the door. They have a sense of safety and security because they are well grounded in the Bible, but they are missing the dynamic of living the Spirit-led life.

## Walking the Tightrope

On my daily radio talk show I interviewed renowned Reformed theologian Dr. J. I. Packer. We discussed the conflict that exists between those who promote solid theology and those who teach spiritual experience. His comments were excellent and are worthy of our attention. He said:

> I see as I look around today that there are too many people who are too ready to say that God has given me this, that, and the other vision and that they got a word from the Lord. They cheerfully say it but they don't lay it before the church for testing; they just go ahead and do it, and sometimes they come an awful cropper. There is this great section of the church, as we all know, which is very high on the ministry of the Holy Spirit in the heart of the individual. Among those folks, all kinds of notions are set forth as to

what God said to me, and what I got from the Lord, and what I must do and so forth. . . . There is that extreme. And on the other side of the tightrope walk is the opposite extreme. They say, "No, no, all God's guidance come to us from direct inference from the Bible" and application of what's written, and it's a matter of common sense, and sober thought . . . and they come to the point of saying that there isn't such a thing as the nudge of God in the heart. Well, I spoke of a tightrope walk and maybe you can see what my idea is. Being a practical Christian is in so many ways like walking a tightrope. You are always in danger of losing your balance and falling off either to the right hand or to the left. . . . I believe one loses more by denying that there is such a thing as the nudge of the Holy Spirit than pouring in any amount of common sense and business as usual.[4]

## Correct, Not Reject!

There is no doubt that the dimension of spiritual experience is replete with potential pitfalls, but should that dimension be rejected or *corrected?*

Christian truth is balanced truth. Error in the church is often not the lack of truth, but truth that is out of proportion with other truth. Heresy is often truth pushed to an extreme. Think, for example, about the importance of striking the proper balance between the Law and the Gospel, faith and works, or God's sovereignty and man's will.

While an overt emphasis upon the Law might dangerously undermine the Gospel, that doesn't mean we should reject the role of the Law in the life of a Christian.

While an overt emphasis upon good works might put us in danger of obscuring the truth that salvation is by faith alone, that doesn't mean we should stop teaching the necessity of good works as the fruit of our faith.

While an overt emphasis upon the human will might cause us to stop relying on God's sovereign grace, that doesn't mean we should stop emphasizing the role of the will in living the Christian life lest we become mere robots.

Balance is needed when we deal with the relationship between sound theology and inner spiritual experience. There is no reason why charismatic and Pentecostal churches cannot have good theology. And there is no reason why traditional, doctrinally sound churches cannot place an emphasis upon spiritual experience.

A wise man once said, "If you have solid theology and no experience, you dry up. If you have spiritual experience and bad theology, you blow up. But if you have good theology together with spiritual experience, you grow up!"

There are many mainline, denominational churches with good theology that have dried up.

There are many charismatic fellowships with an emphasis on spiritual experience that have blown up.

Is it not time for us to grow up?

Is it possible to maintain sound biblical theology
and still leave room for spiritual experience
without creating confusion? Yes! But both
elements of Christianity must be put into
their proper context.

# 4

# Can Doctrine and Experience Walk Together?

Is it possible to reconcile sound biblical doctrine and inner spiritual experience without creating confusion? Yes it is, but to do so we must be willing to make a clear distinction between *what we know* based upon Scripture and *what we believe or think we know* based upon our experience. *We must distinguish biblical doctrine from spiritual experience.*

## Replacing Confusion with Clarity

Let us attempt to make a clear distinction between two aspects of the Christian life: *doctrine and experience.*

Christian doctrine or teaching defines what we believe about God, creation, man, sin, salvation, and so on. Doctrine is drawn from and based upon the clear teaching of Scripture. God is at the center of Christian doctrine. We search the Word of God to discover what God has done for us as our creator, redeemer, and sanctifier.

The defining truth of Christian doctrine is the message of the cross of Jesus Christ. I know that my sins are forgiven. I know that I am right with God. I know that I have eternal life in heaven because the Bible tells me that God sent his Son into this world to die for me. He has promised that hearing that message of salvation will produce faith.

Christian doctrine is secure. When it comes to the forgiveness of my sins and my eternal salvation, what I think, feel, or experience makes absolutely no difference. No matter how the devil might seek to accuse me, the fact is, Jesus gave his life for me and shed his blood on the cross. Therefore, my sins are forgiven. There is no doubt about it; I have eternal life.

Spiritual experience, on the other hand, while confirmed by the promise and precedent of God's Word, is based upon feelings and emotions. So when I say that I believe the Holy Spirit has led me to write this book, I am not stating a Christian doctrine. There are no biblical promises that the Holy Spirit at this time and place would direct me to write a book. Yet, in sensing the spiritual dynamic that is going on within me, I believe he has. This is my opinion or my feeling about the matter, even if you choose not to agree with me.

Doctrinal statements are based upon the clear, objective acts of God revealed in the Bible. They are secure and definite. Statements about our spiritual experiences, derived from the precedent of Scripture, are based upon personal feelings. Because our feelings are changeable, they are not secure. They are not definite. But they are most certainly believable.

If you believe that you have experienced some form of the power and presence of the Holy Spirit in your life, it is not my intention to undermine your feelings. It is my hope, as a result of reading this book, that you will establish your relationship with God, your forgiveness, your righteousness, and your eternal salvation upon the solid foundation of God's eternal Word, not upon your feelings. But in so doing, I do not want to discourage you from discerning the "nudge of the Spirit" in your daily decision-making.

On the other hand, I am not seeking to throw a monkey wrench into anyone's systematic theology. What I am about to share with you is not intended to be codified nor engraved in stone. If you choose to embrace and put into practice some of the principles I share with you, it will not change your theology, but it may change your life.

Let's begin by applying the difference between biblical doctrine and spiritual experience to the controversial phenomenon of speaking in tongues.

## A Balanced Perspective

The Bible teaches that there is an experience called *glossolalia,* or speaking in tongues. I know that Peter, Paul, and the rest of the apostles spoke in tongues because the Bible says they did. There is biblical precedent. The Bible does not say that people in every age would speak in tongues, but neither does it say that they wouldn't. On this issue, the Bible is silent.

So how do charismatics know that the unintelligible words and phrases they utter is speaking in tongues? They know because charismatic teachers, on the basis of biblical precedent combined with their own experience, taught them what speaking in tongues was, how it worked, how you come into it, and what to expect from it.

Are people today speaking in tongues? If we hold to the reformers' observation that Scripture alone is the basis for all doctrinal truth concerning life and salvation, the best we can say is maybe so. But then again, maybe not!

There is nothing wrong with charismatics believing that the unknown words and phrases they utter in their devotional life is "praying in the Spirit" or speaking in tongues as long as they place their experience into a proper context. They must make a clear distinction between doctrinal, truth-based Scripture and experience based upon feelings. I have known many charismatics who claim to speak in tongues, but at times have their doubts as to whether or not they are speaking tongues in the same way that Peter, James, John and Paul did. That is understandable. But would you want to put your beliefs about your forgiveness of sins and eternal salvation into the same category as your beliefs about speaking in tongues?

## Personal Piety

Every Christian denomination has its own brand of piety and devotion. For example, if you do some TV "channel surfing," you may encounter a Roman Catholic worship service in which the participants wear elaborate robes, chant, make the sign of the cross, and use the historic liturgy as their basis for worship. If you continue through the channels, you may find yourself in the midst of a black Pentecostal worship service, which will be quite different. Is one brand of piety necessarily better than another brand, or is it a matter of choice? The dictionary defines *piety* as "religious fervor, exercise, or practice." Another word for piety is *devotion*.

I had a man in one of my former congregations tell me that when he sits in church and looks up at the cross, the Holy Spirit is stirred within him and he feels close to the Lord. Is he allowed to feel this way even though there is no biblical promise that sitting in church and looking up at a cross will stir up the Holy Spirit? Of course he is. If that is what he feels, who am I to argue with him?

Responsible charismatic leaders must grapple with the relationship between Christian doctrine based on Scripture and spiritual experience based on feelings to rid the movement of fraud, deception, and danger. The Holy Spirit would not clearly reveal the truth of "Scripture alone" to the reformers in the sixteenth century and then change his mind in the twentieth century.

But on the other hand, doctrine-minded Christians must be careful not to be critical of the piety that is evidenced within the varied groupings of God's people. Since Scripture is silent, it is just as wrong for the opponents of the charismatic movement to claim that speaking in tongues does not exist today. Is it possible that they are basing their claim on their personal opinions and their lack of experience?

## Leaving Room for Uncertainty

When we evaluate our inner experiences, we are always in the dimension of uncertainty. Of course, when we follow biblical direction and examine the fruit of our experience we can very well conclude in all probability that it was from the Holy Spirit, but there will always be some element of doubt. For this reason, when we declare the leading of the Spirit in our lives, we should say, "The Lord told me, I think."

If we attempt to move our experience out of the realm of uncertainty and into the realm of knowledge, we fall into the same error as Benny Hinn, who fails to distinguish doctrinal truth based upon Scripture from experience based upon feelings. Hinn writes, "You should never doubt the leading of the Holy Spirit."[1]

I agree wholeheartedly. If I knew I was being led by the Holy Spirit, I would not doubt. The question is, how do I know whether or not the Holy Spirit is leading me?

What does the Bible say? Does the Bible teach us to expect a definite "hotline to heaven"? Did the apostles have such a hotline?

## A Puzzle

When he wrote to the Corinthians, the apostle Paul said that our knowledge is imperfect. We see partially as if through a glass darkly. The Greek word used in that verse is *enigma*, which means "puzzle." This describes the condition we encounter when we attempt to discern the leading of the Holy Spirit.

This condition, in fact, applied to the apostle Paul himself. He also saw the leading of the Holy Spirit through a "glass darkly." I would be so bold to suggest that there were times when Paul actually "blew it" so to speak. He may have had times when he thought he was being led by the Holy Spirit only to find out later that he was following his own imagination.

For the Holy Spirit to have led the apostles in a clear and precise manner it would have been necessary to eliminate the working of the devil, the world, and the sinful flesh, since these alternative sources cloud the Spirit's guidance. If these hindrances had been eliminated, the apostles would have been certain that every thought, insight, dream, or vision they received was from above.

## Apostolic Conflict

Scripture, however, affirms that the apostles weren't always clear about the Spirit's leading. Consider the heated disagreement that arose between Paul and Barnabas over whether or not to take John Mark with them on their second missionary journey (Acts 15:36-41). The disagreement was so intense it produced a division between them. Paul took Silas and traveled to Lystra and Derbe, and Barnabas took Mark and sailed for Cyprus. If Paul and Barnabas had a "hotline to heaven" and clear guidance from the Holy Spirit, their disagreement could have been avoided.

Perhaps they went their separate ways and were both being led by the Holy Spirit. Maybe God wanted to multiply the ministry. If they had a hotline to heaven, they should have known this and decided to part company without the major contention.

Consider the conflict that arose between Peter and Paul at Antioch (Galatians 2:11-21). Was Peter led by the Holy Spirit when he refused to eat with the Gentiles? Obviously not! Was Paul led by the Holy Spirit when he confronted Peter in front of the entire assembly rather than first dealing with him privately? Perhaps not.

## Learning to Use Discernment

Why did the apostles believe that some thoughts, ideas, insights, dreams, visions, or prophetic utterances were from the Holy Spirit? Not every thought entertained by an evangelist or an apostle was from the Holy Spirit. There are other possible sources. Dreamers, visionaries, and prophets might be eccentrics. Not all who claimed to be speaking the will of God were doing so. Why would Paul instruct the early Christians to test prophecy with discernment (1 Thessalonians 5:21)? And how did this discernment work?

The first-century Christians understood the conflict that existed between the devil, the world, the sinful nature, and the Holy Spirit. They learned to discern as best as they could. They knew that their knowledge was imperfect and incomplete. They were seeing the will of God through a glass darkly. Even though it was a puzzle, they didn't give up and merely resort to unaided human reason and common sense. Nor did they fall into the trap of thinking that every dream, thought, or figment of their imagination was from the Holy Spirit.

As you read and study the teaching sections of the New Testament, primarily the epistles, you will discover insights on the following subjects:

1. Distinguishing the flesh from the Spirit.
2. Being filled with the Holy Spirit.
3. Having your thoughts and impressions renewed by setting your mind on the things of the Spirit.
4. Discerning circumstances that might confirm your impressions.
5. Being led by the Spirit produces peace and not confusion.

6. Receiving guidance from other members of the body of Christ as you move together in ministry.

Because these early Christians understood the conflict, they trained their minds to discern the voice of the Holy Spirit. They developed the ability—even though it was imperfect—to distinguish the devil, the world, and the flesh from the Holy Spirit. They were like the mature Christians described in Hebrews 5:14; they had trained their senses to discern right from wrong. We need to do that today as well. We need to, as 2 Corinthians 10:5 says, take every thought captive to the obedience of Christ.

The first-century Christians learned how to be led by the Holy Spirit. We need to do the same, even though we will never get to the point, this side of heaven, of having perfect knowledge.

## Why Bother?

If we can never be certain that our impressions, thoughts, insights, visions, or dreams are definitely from the Holy Spirit and be able to declare with doctrinal certainty, "The Lord told me," or "The Lord is leading me," then why bother? Would it not be better to operate on the basis of reason or common sense, do that which seems right to us on the basis of biblical inference, and let the Holy Spirit operate behind the scenes?

No, that would not be right. The Bible commands us to be led by the Spirit. God is our heavenly Father and we are his children. Our Father in heaven knows that in spiritual matters, we are not very bright. We are children. The Bible says that in matters of the Holy Spirit, our thoughts, our knowledge, our reasoning is childish (1 Corinthians 13:11).

Jesus called us sheep who listen to his voice, but sheep are not sharp animals.

Jesus compared our heavenly Father to earthly fathers. Would an earthly father refuse to teach his child to learn how to ride a bike because the child will fall off? Would an earthly father refuse to teach his child to play baseball because the child will on some occasions strike out or make an error? Of course not!

I believe it is displeasing to our Father in heaven when we act as if we have inside information as to what he is up to in our world and give the impression that we have already discovered his will. It is offensive to our Father in heaven when we say, "The Lord told me" if in fact he didn't tell us. We need to walk humbly, as children, before our Father in heaven.

I believe it is also displeasing to our Father in heaven when we make decisions concerning our lives, his church, and the work of his kingdom without any conscious sensitivity to what his will might be or how the Holy Spirit might be leading. Are our thoughts the same as his thoughts? Is our will the same as his will? Is our wisdom the same as his wisdom? Because we happen to have a diploma on our wall, a degree after our name, or a position in his church does not make our plans his plans. The apostle Paul writes, "Who has known the mind of the Lord that he may instruct him?" (1 Corinthians 2:16).

## Get Into the Game!

When we play baseball, it's possible that we may strike out or make an error. It is also possible that we may hit a home run. That's what makes the game exciting—there is uncertainty.

This is equally true when you seek to be led by the Spirit. We may bang our heads on closed doors and get bumps on our forehead, but eventually one door might open. What we think is the Holy Spirit might be our imagination. But then again, it might be the Holy Spirit. We may be led into an exciting work. Will we make mistakes? Yes! Can we ever be absolutely certain? No! But at least we are "in the game." That is what our Father in heaven wants us to do: Get in the game. Are you ready?

Being led by the Spirit means to follow the guidance of the Spirit—not the guidance of the devil, the world, and the old sinful nature. This relates not only to fighting sinful impulses, but personal decision-making as well. Being led is not a strange, mystical dynamic.

# 5

# What Does It Mean to Be Led By the Spirit?

We know from the four Gospels that our Lord Jesus was led by the Holy Spirit.

We know from the book of Acts that the Holy Spirit led the Apostles.

Yet, there is no teaching in either the Gospels or in the book of Acts defining and explaining the manner in which that guidance took place. We *know* that the Holy Spirit led Jesus and the apostles, but we don't exactly know *how* he did it. (The exception, of course, is when the book of Acts reveals the Spirit's working through dreams, visions, angels, and prophets.)

However, the epistles tell us about being led by the Spirit. The two main Scripture passages on this subject are Romans 8 and Galatians 5.

In Romans 8:12-14, we read:

Therefore, brothers, we have an obligation—but it is not to the sinful nature, to live according to it. For if you live according to the sinful nature, you will die; but if by the Spirit you put to death the misdeeds of the body, you will live, because those *who are led by the Spirit of God* are sons of God (emphasis added).

And in Galatians 5:17-18, Paul tells us:

The sinful nature desires what is contrary to the Spirit, and the Spirit what is contrary to the sinful nature. They are in conflict with each other, so that you do not do what you want. *But if you are led by the Spirit,* you are not under law (emphasis added).

## Led by the Spirit

What does it means to be led by the Spirit?

When the apostle Paul speaks about "the Spirit," he makes no distinction between the Holy Spirit and the human spirit. Some people have attempted to clarify this distinction. I follow the principle that if an issue is unclear in Scripture, it is unclear for a reason—possibly because it does not make a great deal of difference one way or other. We know that the Holy Spirit is joined to our human spirit (Romans 8:16) probably in the same way tea is mixed into water. When you take a sip of tea, you are unable to distinguish the tea from the water. In the same way, we are unable to distinguish the Holy Spirit from the human spirit.

Bible teachers generally agree that when the apostle Paul tells us to be led by the Spirit, he is not speaking of some momentary external invasion of the Holy Spirit into our consciousness, telling us what to do and how to do it. Nor is he referring to our effort to conjure up the Spirit in some mystical encounter. Paul is simply telling us to live according to our new life in Christ, which is Christ dwelling within us by his Holy Spirit, or to be "led by the Spirit" as opposed to living according to our old sinful nature, or being "led by the flesh."

## Does This Just Involve Avoiding Sin?

Many of the evangelical authors who have written on the subject of guidance by and large seek to downplay the notion of the Holy Spirit leading via the inward guidance of our thoughts and impressions. They probably want to avoid any hint of mysticism. They interpret "led by the Spirit" in Romans 8:14 and Galatians 5:18 as having only moral implication; the Spirit fights against our desires to sin. For example, Dr. J. I. Packer, in his book *Hot Tub Religion,* writes:

> What does it mean to be "led by the Spirit?" That phrase, found in Romans 8:14 and Galatians 5:18, speaks of resisting sinful impulses, *not of decision making* (emphasis added). [1]

In an edition of the *Reformation Canada* journal, Roger Fellows wrote an article on the subject of knowing God's will. He makes the following statements about the interpretation of Romans 8:14 and Galatians 5:18:

> The statement (in Romans 8:14) about being led by the Spirit . . . deals with putting to death the misdeeds of the body. Mortification of sin is an indispensable part of being led by the Spirit. That removes "leading" from the realm of the subjective into the area of sanctification. The Spirit leads us in holiness and warfare against sin as we obey God's Word.

Commenting on the Galatians 5 text, Fellows writes:

> The whole context of verses 16-25 has to do with moral behavior rather than a subjective sense of guidance. Being led by the Spirit means manifesting the fruit of the Spirit, and avoiding the works of the sinful nature. [2]

There is no doubt that the command to be "led by the Spirit" has moral implications. It's true that Paul is talking about living the Christian life and avoiding the impulses of the old sinful nature. But I have great difficulty, both biblically and experientially, separating moral behavior or resisting sinful impulses from subjective decision-making. I believe that when it comes to seeking the will of God for our lives, the two are interrelated.

Let's say, for example, I am walking down a city street and I pass by an adult bookstore. My old sinful nature is stirred and I am tempted to enter so that I can indulge the wants of the sinful flesh. The Holy Spirit dwelling within me goes to work. He impresses upon me that I am putting my spiritual life in danger and purposely seeking to live contrary to the will of God. As a result, I will lose my joy and peace. The Spirit contends with the desires of the sinful flesh. But I am a new Christian, weak in faith, and I give in to the temptation.

But let's change the scenario a bit and imagine that I am two blocks away from the adult bookstore. As I am walking, I come to a corner where I must decide whether to go straight or to turn left. If I go straight, I'll pass the adult bookstore. Now I have a decision to make. Might not the Holy Spirit, who knows that I am a weak Christian, urge me to turn left so that I would not walk past the adult bookstore and therefore avoid the temptation?

Of course, there is a difference in how we would categorize the Spirit's work in those situations. I know for a fact, because the Bible says so, that the Holy Spirit will fight against the temptation to sin. But to believe that the Holy Spirit is leading you to make a left turn as you are walking down the street is within the realm of personal piety. There is no certainty that the impression is from the Holy Spirit. But, if you later discover that your left-hand turn directed you away from the adult book-store, you would have a good confirmation that the impression was from the Holy Spirit. Yet, that would still fall in the realm of personal piety and not Bible-based faith.

Taking our thoughts a step further, many of the decisions that we ponder are not always explicit choices between sinful and non-sinful acts. If they were, the issue of guidance would be a simple matter. Very often our desires, even though on the surface they may appear to be good, are motivated by self or the world. The devil works hard to get us to do our own thing, even though "our own thing" might not be blatantly sinful.

That's why I maintain the position that being "led by the Spirit" in Romans 8:14 and Galatians 5:18 not only refers to fighting sinful impulses but also personal decision-making. (As we continue through this book I will offer more support for this perspective.) I believe that we severely hamstring the Body of Christ when we attempt to separate the Holy Spirit's work of keeping us from sinning and his work of guiding our lives.

## Is This a Mystical Experience?

Is the experience of being led by the Spirit as seen in Romans and Galatians the same experience that the apostles had when they were led by the Spirit in the book of Acts? Are we looking at two different dynamics—one having to do with our natural, inward, moral choices and the other an external, supernatural, mystical invasion of the Holy Spirit into the apostolic consciousness? Or are they the same dynamic?

When Christians speak about being led by thoughts or impressions from the Holy Spirit, some people interpret that to mean that they are promoting a supernatural, mystical encounter with the Spirit. For example, in his otherwise excellent book, *Knowing God's Will*, M. Blaine Smith writes:

> Then there is the area of inward guidance—guidance through mystical impressions. This is an extremely popular approach to God's will, and one which needs to be put in careful perspective. . . . What is common . . . is the belief that God speaks directly through our feelings—that is, that our intuition is the direct voice of the Holy Spirit.[3]

In that brief quote, Blaine Smith, by using the phrases "mystical impressions," "God speaks directly," and "direct voice of the Holy Spirit," places the subject of inward guidance into the context of strange and supernatural experiences. This is most certainly not the case.

If we want to understand how it is that the Holy Spirit leads us by thoughts and impressions, it helps to think of the manner in which we are led by our sinful nature, the devil, and the world. Those are our enemies. They are the alternative to being led by the Spirit.

We all know what it means to be pushed by our sinful nature. Who has not experienced selfish motives, sinful thoughts, the lusts of the flesh? Are you immune from thoughts of self-pity, anger, or resentment? Have you ever made decisions because it was best for you and it furthered your plans and ambitions without any regard for anyone else? From where did these notions arise, if not from your old sinful nature?

We all know what it means to be tempted and seduced by the devil. What Christian has not experienced temptation? Some of the ideas that enter into our minds . . . are they not at times injected by the devil?

We know what it means to be drawn away by the desires of the world. Who has not watched television or shopped in a glitzy department stores and experienced the alluring, covetous tug of the things of this world?

In the same manner, Paul is telling us in Romans and Galations to be internally guided by the Spirit or by our new life in Christ Jesus. He is speaking of an *internal guidance system.*

Some people will respond to that concept by saying that this internal guidance system implies some strange, mystical encounter. But it's interesting that when we speak of thoughts that are initiated by the devil, stirred by the sinful nature, or prompted by the allure of the world, we don't call them strange and mystical encounters. These are a part of our fleshly makeup.

Is not the Holy Spirit also a part of the internal makeup of a Christian? If we can receive thoughts from the devil, the world, and the sinful flesh, should we not also expect contrasting thoughts from the Spirit of God dwelling within us?

I believe that the manner in which the apostles were led by the Spirit in the book of Acts is the same as that taught by the apostle Paul in his epistles. The only difference between Christians in the first century and Christians today is that the Christians in the first century were taught how to be led by the Spirit. Today, there is very little teaching on this subject.

## Putting What We Learn into Action

Having set the stage, let us now become practical. We will look at what the Bible says about being led by the Spirit and examine the following issues:

1. Distinguishing the flesh from the Spirit.
2. Being filled with the Holy Spirit.
3. Having your mind renewed.
4. Setting your mind on the things of the Spirit and discerning your impressions and ideas.
5. Looking for the circumstances that might confirm your impressions.
6. God is the author of peace, not confusion.
7. Listening to other members of the Body of Christ.
8. Guidance is a process.
9. Moving together in ministry.
10. Stepping out in faith!

The first step in seeking to be led by
the Spirit is to be able to distinguish the flesh,
that is, the old sinful nature, from the Spirit, that
is, the new life in Christ.

# 6

# Conflict as We Walk in the Spirit

Before you can understand what it means to be led by the Spirit, you must first understand your makeup. Who are you? What makes you tick? What influences your decisions?

You were born into this world as a selfish sinner. That is your inheritance from Adam. Your thoughts were motivated by your selfish sinful nature. You made your life-decisions based on what was best for you or what you wanted. Your concern was to advance your position in the world. Perhaps you did your own thing or followed the principle, "If it feels good, do it."

Then you became a Christian. The Holy Spirit brought you to faith in Jesus Christ. You became a new creature. You were born-again. You received new spiritual life. The life of Christ, by the Holy Spirit, actually entered into you. "If anyone is in Christ," Paul writes, "he is a new creation. The old has gone, the new has come!" (2 Corinthians 5:17). In John 3, Jesus told Nicodemus, "You must be born again." He explained to Nicodemus that a person can neither see nor enter the Kingdom of God, the place where

God rules, unless he receives a new spiritual life. Peter writes, "You have been born again, not of perishable seed, but of imperishable, through the living and enduring word of God" (1 Peter 1:23). Your new life in Christ Jesus produces a new motivation. There is a new source affecting your mind, but . . .

## Your Sinful Nature Still Exists!

There are many Christians who refuse to accept the biblical truth that their sinful nature still exists and influences their actions, thoughts, and will. They say, "I was once a sinner, but I am no longer a sinner." They proceed to make the mistake of identifying their conflicting thoughts as either emanating from the Holy Spirit or from the devil. They perceive that the conflicts within are not caused by the continued existence of their sinful nature.

Most mainline Protestant Christians who embrace the biblical understanding that came out of the sixteenth-century Reformation have no difficulty accepting the continued existence of the sinful nature in the life of a Christian. It is a vital and integral part of their systematic understanding of how the Law and Gospel function as well as the nature of both justification and sanctification.

If you have been influenced by alternative teaching and embrace the notion that you are no longer a sinner and that your sinful nature no longer exists, I would encourage you to read Appendix 2 in the back of the book. The continued existence of the sinful nature is an important issue that not only impacts the manner in which we regard ourselves but also the manner in which we regard the righteousness of Christ.

If I do not acknowledge that sin still dwells within my heart and mind and has an influence upon me, I can easily fall into the trap of thinking that all my thoughts are God's thoughts, all my ideas are God's and all my intentions are his as well. The only way I could go wrong is if the devil gets a hold of me.

For example, some years ago a popular televangelist got caught in his immorality. He stood before his television audience with tears flowing down his cheeks and said, "I don't know what happened to me."

From where I was sitting, it was obvious what had happened to him: He had given in to the desires of his old sinful nature. He was not led by the Spirit, but by his sinful nature. He demonstrated clearly that he was a sinner. But he refused to admit this. He said that he wasn't the problem. The devil made him do it; he had demons within. Another televangelist then came along and supposedly cast the demons out of him, but it did no good.

What the televangelist needed to do was recognize the reality of his sinful nature, receive some understanding as to the causes and effect of that old sinful nature, and learn how to walk in the Spirit. Then he might have been able to control his problems. Instead, he said, "The devil made me do it." That is a cop-out.

## Five Minutes Can Make a Difference

It is amazing how quickly our thoughts and actions can move from being influenced by the Spirit to being influenced by the old sinful nature.

For example, one Sunday morning I enjoyed a beautiful worship experience. The singing, the choir, had been magnificent. I had preached on my favorite subject—justification. And it seemed that the words just poured out of me. As I walked home from church at noon, I felt like I was walking on air. The joy and peace remained and bubbled over as an afterglow of the worship experience.

When I got home I greeted my wife Dianne, who was busy preparing the Sunday dinner.

"Wasn't that a great service?" I asked, fully expecting a positive response. Dianne was often sensitive to the quality of the worship service and the response of the congregation. Oftentimes she will say, "Wow, the worship was fantastic. Wasn't the choir great? . . ."

"I didn't get anything out of it," she snapped.

"What do you mean you didn't get anything out of it? The worship was fantastic, and you didn't get anything out of it? How in the world could anyone sit in that church this morning and not get anything out of it?. . ."

"Oh, it's easy for you," she interrupted. "You are not stuck balancing a baby on your lap, juggling the hymnal, and trying to break up an argument between the other kids. I don't understand why our kids can't behave in church. They are always at each other. I get so mad sometimes I could scream."

My blood began to boil. I got up from the kitchen table and marched into the living room, where the Sunday paper was scattered all over the floor. The two older kids were on the floor reading pages from the comic section.

"What's the matter with you two?" I asked in anger. "Why can't you behave in church? You got your mother all upset."

"He keeps teasing me," my older daughter said while, pointing her finger at my oldest son, who usually got the blame for most of the family squabbles and often rightly so.

"Get out of here, both of you! Go to your rooms!" I took them by their arms and marched them into their rooms and slammed the doors. Then I went back into the living room and angrily began gathering the papers together.

Amazingly, within about five minutes, the joy, peace, and sense of excitement that had been flowing within me as a result of a wonderful worship experience had been replaced with anger and frustration. While my preaching a little while earlier might have been led by the Spirit, my response to my kids was definitely led by the flesh. What a difference five minutes can make!

I'm sure you've encountered a similar situation. All Christians go through experiences of this nature. They may feel great one moment, lifted up into the heavenly places, and suddenly come crashing down the next moment when they are again confronted with the reality of the old sinful nature. That's to be expected in the Christian life.

## Two Sources of Guidance

There are two sources of guidance that can influence our thoughts and attitudes. These two sources are in conflict with each other. We were born into this world in Adam, and the old nature of Adam was joined to us. Later on when we came to faith in Jesus Christ, we were born again in Christ and his life was joined to us. This is our condition.

As the result of our "double birth" in Adam and in Christ, while we are still upon this earth, we possess, in a sense, a double life. Paul refers to this double life as being "the old man" and "the new man," or the flesh (the sinful human nature) and the Spirit (Christ dwelling within). The life of Adam, which is *our human* life, will continue to adhere to us until we bury "the earthly man" in the dust from whence he came. The new life of Christ, which also dwells within us, is an *alien* life. It comes from a different world. It is the life of "the heavenly man" (1 Corinthians 15: 46-49).

Because of this "double life," the normal Christian experience of seeking to do the will of God is a struggle.

I cannot tell you how many Christians I have met who bemoan that they still have conflicts and are battling the thoughts and temptations that arise from the old sinful nature. The truth is, conflict is normal. I believe one of the greatest evidences that a person is a Christian is the presence of conflict. Those who are not believers in Jesus Christ do not have the Holy Spirit; therefore, they experience no conflict.

If a Christian does *not* experience conflict in his decision-making process, it is possible that he has given in to doing "what comes naturally" or following the principle, "If it feels good, do it."

## Walking in the Spirit

Seeking to be led by the Holy Spirit simply means that we live according to our new life in Christ and not according to our old life in Adam. Understanding this is not difficult. Paul writes, "Just as you received Christ Jesus as Lord, continue to live in him" (Colossians 2:6). In his 1535 commentary on the book of Galatians, Martin Luther paraphrases Paul's words in Galatians 5:16 by saying:

> The Spirit struggles against the flesh and the flesh against the Spirit. All I am requiring of you now—and for that matter, all you are able to produce—is that you follow the guidance of the Spirit and resist the guidance of the flesh.[1]

In Romans 6:4, Paul wrote, "We were therefore buried with him through baptism into death in order that, just as Christ was raised from the dead through the glory of the Father, we too may live a new life." In his famous *Small Catechism*, Martin Luther explains Paul's words under the heading "The Significance of Baptism":

> It signifies that the Old Adam in us, by daily contrition and repentance, be drowned and die with all sins and evil lusts and, again, a new man daily come forth and arise, who shall live before God in righteousness and purity forever.

## "Adam, Where Are You?"

While the concept of walking in and being led by the Spirit is actually quite simple, the difficulty arises when we attempt to identify which of our thoughts are of Adam and which are of Christ. As we attempt to discern our thoughts, insights, and ideas, we should ask ourselves this question: "Does this come from the flesh or from the Spirit?"

The difficulty in identifying our old sinful nature is simple: We don't want to do it! We don't want to question our thoughts, ideas, intentions, and desires and arrive at the conclusion that what we are thinking and what we have set our heart upon is coming from our old sinful nature. It is a blow to our pride. We're afraid that our self-esteem might be injured. Just as Adam hid himself from God after he fell into sin, so also does our old sinful nature want to remain hidden from sight.

I have met some people who camouflage "ol' Adam" behind a spiritual veneer. This is a common deception that I have often fallen into myself. I knew one man, for example, who was never able to hold down a job. After being "spiritually renewed," he claimed that it was the Lord who was leading him from one occupation to another. In prayer meetings he would stand up and tell people about the new opportunities the "Lord" was opening up for him. But when we looked at his life, we could see that nothing had changed. He had merely given his impetuous, old sinful nature a coat of paint.

There was another man I had known for years who was demanding of the people around him. He always wanted to be the expert and tell other people how to think and live. When he became "spiritual," his "gift of advice" was simply renamed "practicing spiritual discernment." The "ol' Adam" remained in hiding.

In another instance, after I had been in the ministry for three years, I received a call to become the pastor of another congregation. They offered more money. The parsonage was bigger. I knew that making the move into a larger church would provide me with greater personal prestige. So I accepted the call. Of course, when I explained my decision to the congregation where I was serving, I spoke of the greater ministry opportunities. I whitewashed ol' Adam. Don't we all do that?

If we desire to be led by the Spirit and not by the flesh, ol' Adam must be exposed.

## Works and Fruit

The Bible gives to us a clear way of determining whether we're being guided by our old sinful nature or our new life in Christ—the flesh or the Spirit. We can identify the source by looking at the results of the guidance.

In Galatians, Paul provides ample evidence to help us determine whether we are being led by the old sinful nature or the new life in Christ. He writes:

The acts of the sinful nature are obvious: sexual immorality, impurity and debauchery; idolatry and witchcraft; hatred, discord, jealousy, fits of rage, selfish ambition, dissensions, factions and envy; drunkenness, orgies, *and the like* (Galatians 5:19-21, emphasis added).

The key words in that text are "and the like." The list is unending. You can add resentment, bitterness, self-pity, self-centeredness, confusion, chaos, arrogance, worry, fear, discontentment, impetuousness, stubbornness, intolerance, and so on.

In contrast, Paul tells us that . . .

The fruit of the Spirit is love, joy, peace, patience, kindness, goodness, faithfulness, gentleness and self-control (Galatians 5:22-23).

So, there are two forces battling for the control of your life and influencing the way you think: the flesh and the Spirit. For this reason, seeking to be led by the Spirit is not easy. Your old sinful nature, though dead and buried, remains stubborn and most certainly has a mind of its own.

## Always a Mixture

Even if you learn to make a clearer distinction between the flesh and the Spirit, please understand that none of your actions will be purely of the flesh or the Spirit. There is always a mixture. For example, you might sin, have your conscience bother you, and be led by the Spirit into repentance. Or, as you seek to live in the Spirit, you might become proud or critical of those whom you perceive as living in the flesh. I know a man who claims that the Lord has led him through some difficult times. He has, as he puts it, "been broken before the Lord." He often speaks of his humility. The problem is, he seems to be a little too proud of the fact that he is humble. So there is a mixture present within him.

As you seek to be led by the Spirit, you must always be conscious of the continued existence of your sinful nature. You may begin with your thoughts and actions primarily in the Spirit and wind up in the flesh. While the conflict will always exist, the Bible commands us to be led by the Spirit, walk in the Spirit, and be filled with the Spirit.

Being filled with the Spirit is not a description
of how much of the Holy Spirit we happen to have.
Rather, it is a description of the quality of our life.
The Bible teaches us
how to be filled with the Spirit.

# 7

# Filled with the Spirit

W hat is the Bible saying when it talks about being filled with the Spirit or describes a person as full of the Spirit? In the book of Acts, the apostles were filled with the Holy Spirit (2:4; 4:31), Peter was filled (4:8), Ananias told Saul to be filled (9:17), and on the first missionary journey Saul is described as being filled (13:9). One of the requirements for the deacons chosen in chapter six was that they be full of the Holy Spirit (6:3), Stephen was full of the Holy Spirit (7:55), and Barnabas was full as well (11:24).

## Quality of Life, Not Quantity of Spirit

The term "filled with the Holy Spirit" is often thought of as a quantitative phrase that describes how much of the Holy Spirit a person happens to possess. I heard one Bible teacher declare, "I need to be continually filled with the Holy Spirit because I leak." He was saying that he uses up the Holy Spirit similar to the way his car uses up gasoline. Just as he needs to go to the gas station to fill up his car, so also does he need to continually pray that God will fill him with the Holy Spirit.

Some people think that being filled with the Holy Spirit is an experience or event communicated by prayer and the laying on of hands. It has been said, "When you are saved, you get the Holy Spirit. The second experience is to be filled with the Holy Spirit." Other people talk about "breathing in the Holy Spirit"—of being filled with the Spirit by faith. These are faulty views.

First, the Holy Spirit is a person, not a temporary, nebulous force that is somehow able to leak out of us. When you receive the Holy Spirit, you receive the entire person. Therefore, when the Bible speaks of being "filled with" or "full of" the Holy Spirit, it is a qualitative statement defining the quality of your life, not a quantitative statement defining the amount of the Spirit you possess.

Second, it is clear from Scripture that not every Christian in the early church was full of the Spirit. In Acts 6:3, the church was to select a group of deacons who would minister to some widows. These deacons were to be men who were "known to be full of the Spirit and wisdom." There must have been Christian men who did not fulfill that requirement or else it would not have been mentioned. We can conclude, then, that those who did not qualify were still Christians—they had the Holy Spirit. But they were not known to be *full* of the Holy Spirit.

Third, since the qualification in Acts 6:3 was not based on *lacking* something from God, it had to be the result of Christian growth and maturity and learning how to put off the sinful nature and be filled with the Holy Spirit. The deacons were men who were "known" to be filled with the Spirit. Their life, conversation, actions, and attitudes manifested the fruit of the Spirit, not the works of the flesh.

## Alternative Fillings

To better understand what it means to be filled with the Spirit, it helps to think of what I call "alternative fillings."

I knew a woman who was filled to overflowing with bitterness and resentment. Her daughter-in-law had offended her many years before, and she refused to extend forgiveness. In her conversations she would invariably end up bad-mouthing her daughter-in-law. How did she become filled with such bitterness? Obviously, she made herself that way.

When we describe a woman who is a selfish, self-centered person, we say, "She is really full of herself." If the topic of conversation is not revolving around her and her problems and successes, she appears totally disinterested. Every element of her life is self-directed and self-motivated. The question is, how did she get that way? By focusing her thoughts and desires upon herself.

I knew a man filled with the world. He owned a jewelry store and was fairly wealthy. When I was together with him the conversation always centered on the things of the world. His life was totally motivated by what he owned, what he was planning to buy, how much his cars, "toys," and jewelry were worth, and so on. He was filled with the world. How did he get that way? By continually focusing his thoughts and desires upon the things of the world.

In contrast with those two alternatives, then, what does it mean to be filled with the Holy Spirit, and how do you get that way? Is it God who sovereignly fills us with the Spirit, or does God give us the gift of the Holy Spirit and leave it up to us to be filled?

## Monergism and Synergism

Theologically, when considering the ministry of the Holy Spirit, it is important to make clear distinction between the two categories of justification and sanctification. Justification defines how we come to faith in Jesus Christ. Sanctification defines how we live the Christian life after we have come to faith in Jesus Christ. Our relationship with the Holy Spirit in sanctification is not the same as it is in justification.

It is the singular work of the Holy Spirit to bring us to faith in Jesus Christ. We do not cooperate. We are acted upon by the Spirit as we hear the message of the Gospel. This is called "monergism," or "one work." It means that the Holy Spirit works alone in bringing us to faith, as opposed to the heresy of "synergism," which means "working with." Synergists teach that we work with the Holy Spirit in order to be saved. The heresy of synergism is based upon the denial of the total corruption of the human nature.

When defining the realm of sanctification, there is a legitimate synergism. Because we are born-again and our will has been quickened, God expects us to cooperate with the Holy Spirit in being filled with the Spirit and led by the Spirit.

Being filled with the Spirit and led by the Spirit are not a part of justification in that they pertain to our forgiveness and eternal life, but are sanctification or the experience of the Christian life. If being filled with the Spirit is a part of santification, in which we cooperate with the

Holy Spirit, what is it that we do in order to be filled with the Spirit?

## Be Filled

The Bible commands us to "be filled with the Spirit" (Ephesians 5:18). God has given to us the gift of the Holy Spirit. It is our responsibility to cooperate with him so that we might be filled with the Spirit. Read carefully Paul's words in Ephesians 5:18-21:

> Do not get drunk on wine, which leads to debauchery. Instead, be filled with the Spirit. Speak to one another with psalms, hymns and spiritual songs. Sing and make music in your heart to the Lord, always giving thanks to God the Father for everything, in the name of our Lord Jesus Christ.

While I generally appreciate the New International Version of the Bible, I do feel the above translation of the original Greek text leaves a great deal to be desired, That's because the words "which leads to debauchery" easily give the impression that being filled with the Spirit *leads to* speaking to one another with psalms, hymns, and spiritual songs, rather than saying that speaking psalms, hymns, and spiritual songs causes a person to be filled with the Spirit.

In the original Greek text, the phrase "which leads to debauchery" is more accurately translated "in which is excess" (εν ω εστιν ασωτια). This is the translation used in the KJV Bible. It does not mean that one causes the other. Paul is saying, "In drunkenness is excess." Also, while it is true that the Greek word for "filled" is in the passive voice (πληρουσθε), indicating that it is an action that is done to us, the word translated "speak" in the NIV is not the first word of a new sentence, but is the present participle "speaking" (λαλουντες) The text says, "Be filled ... speaking." We are dealing with a singular action, not a cause and effect.

Notice that Paul is not only commanding us to be filled with the Spirit but he is teaching us how to do it as well: Be filled ... speaking psalms, hymns, spiritual songs, music in your heart, and giving thanks to the Father for everything.

The apostle expresses the same thoughts in Colossians 3:16:

> Let the word of Christ dwell in you richly as you teach and admonish one another with all wisdom, and as you sing psalms, hymns and spiritual songs with gratitude in your hearts to God. And whatever you do, whether in word or deed, do it all in the name of the Lord Jesus, giving thanks to God the Father through him.

Paul is describing a Spirit-filled life. Being thankful, having the Word of Christ dwelling in our hearts, singing spiritual songs unto the Lord, and consciously doing everything in the name of our Lord Jesus causes us to be filled with the Spirit. As a result, our thoughts and impressions will be led by the Spirit.

A Spirit-filled life is not a life that possesses a huge quantity of the Holy Spirit. The Holy Spirit is a person; you either have him or you don't. So the Spirit-filled life is a life in which our thoughts, feelings, emotions, insights, impulses, desires, and decisions are effected, controlled, influenced, and motivated by the Holy Spirit. The same dynamic is true in describing resentment-filled, self-filled, and world-filled lives.

If you are going to be led by the Spirit, you must be filled with the Spirit. Obviously, if you are filled with your self, you will be led by the desires of the self. If you are filled with the world, you will be led by what the world offers. Being led by the Spirit requires being filled with the Spirit.

## The Vital Ingredients

While there is no doubt that hearing the Word of God and gathering around the Lord's Table are vital ingredients in being filled with the Holy Spirit, the Bible also includes music and singing in that dynamic. In his classic commentary on Ephesians, Dr. George Stoeckhardt says the following about the relationship between "spiritual singing" and being filled with the Spirit:

> True, the true means of edification, the specific means of grace through which the Spirit is given, lives, and operates in us, is the Word of God. However, spiritual singing is but a specific form of the use and application of the divine Word. According to Colossians 3:16 mutal teaching and admonition by means of psalms, hymns and spiritual songs are species of "let the Word of Christ dwell among you richly. . . . It is in this manner also, through hymns and songs, that our spiritual life is refreshed and we are *filled with the Spirit* (emphasis added).[1]

The great reformer Martin Luther highly exalted the role of music. Read carefully some of these beautiful statements:

> We can now adduce only this one fact: Experience testifies, that after the Word of God, music alone deserves to be celebrated as mistress and queen of the heart.

And by these emotions men are controlled and often swept away as by their lords. A greater praise of music than this we cannot conceive. For if you want to revive the sad, startle the jovial, encourage the despairing, humble the conceited, pacify the raving, mollify the hate-filled—and who is able to enumerate all the lords of the human heart, I mean the emotions of the heart and the urges which incite a man to all virtues and vices?—what can you find that is more efficacious than music? The Holy Spirit himself honors it as an instrument of his specific office when he testifies in his Holy Scripture that his gifts came upon the prophets through its use, that is, the impulse toward all virtues, as is seen in the case of Elijah; again, that its use drives out Satan, that is, the power which impels toward all vices, as the case of Saul, king of Israel, shows. Not in vain, therefore, do the father and the prophets want nothing more intimately linked to the Word of God than music. From this arise so many hymns and psalms in which the message and the voice act upon the heart and the hearer at the same time.[2]

Luther further states about the effect of music:

Music is God's greatest gift. It has often so stimulated and stirred me that I felt the desire to preach.[3]

If you want to be filled with the Spirit so that you might be led by the Spirit, direct your heart and mind to the things of the Spirit and not to the things of the flesh. Hide the Word of God in your heart, and ... cultivate the practice of singing hymns and psalms and spiritual songs. Be filled with the Spirit!

To have our minds renewed means to have our thoughts and attitudes motivated by our new life in Christ, or the Spirit—not by the old sinful nature, or the flesh.

# 8

# Renewing Your Mind

The Bible is not merely a book of stuffy doctrines and the offer of "pie in the sky in the great by and by." The Word of God clearly teaches us to how to live, think, and make decisions. The principles of guidance taught especially by the apostle Paul are not laws in the sense of the Ten Commandments, but are principles that help you to understand what is happening in your mind as you seek to discover the will of God. In fact, they are very practical principles.

For example, after encouraging the Christians at Rome to walk in the Spirit and not in the flesh, Paul writes in Romans 8:5-6:

> Those who live according to the sinful nature have their minds set on what that nature desires; but those who live in accordance with the Spirit have their minds set on what the Spirit desires. The mind of sinful man is death, but the mind controlled by the Spirit is life and peace.

This theme of setting our conscious thinking upon the things of the Spirit is an important ingredient in the teaching of the apostle Paul. In Philippians 4:8 we read this:

> Whatever is true, whatever is noble, whatever is right, whatever is pure, whatever is lovely, whatever is admirable—if anything is excellent or praiseworthy—think about such things.

Similarly, we read in Colossians 3:1:

> Since then you have been raised with Christ, set your hearts [affections, the desires of the mind] on things above, where Christ is seated at the right hand of God. Set your minds on things above, not on earthly things.

In 2 Corinthians 10:4-5, Paul speaks of the goal of setting our minds on the things of the Spirit. He writes:

> The weapons we fight with are not the weapons of the world. On the contrary, they have divine power to demolish strongholds. We demolish arguments and every pretension that sets itself up against the knowledge of God, and we take captive every thought to make it obedient to Christ.

In Ephesians 4:22-24, Paul instructs us to put off the old man, be made new in the attitudes of our minds, and put on the new man.

It seems to me that the New Testament repeatedly emphasizes that your thoughts are important to the Holy Spirit.

## Discovering God's Will

I believe the New Testament's most important verse about renewing the mind is found in Romans 12:2. There,

Paul writes, "Do not conform any longer to the pattern of this world, but be transformed by the renewing of your mind. Then you will be able to *test and approve* what God's will is—his good, pleasing and perfect will."

The Greek word translated "test and approve" in the NIV is an interesting word—*dokimazo*. The KJV translates it "prove." Elsewhere in the New Testament, *dokimazo* is translated "test, try, discern, examine or discover." The word defines the process of examining, testing, and discerning in order to make a discovery or to determine whether or not something is genuine. For example, in a courtroom, the evidence is examined and tested in order to prove innocence or guilt and thereby reach a verdict.

If you put together all of Paul's teaching about the renewal of the mind, this is what you come up with: Our minds are renewed as we learn to set them upon the things of the Spirit. As our minds are renewed, we will be able—by a process of discerning, examining, and testing—*to discover the will of God.*

## Where It All Begins

Every decision you ever made, every course you ever plotted, every direction you ever chose to follow, every good idea or impression or insight you ever came up with *began in your mind.* Since your mind is at the center of your being, whether you are being led by the Spirit or by your old sinful nature will clearly make a difference in the substance of your thoughts.

Putting it simply, the mind is like a computer. With computers, we say that "garbage in equals garbage out." Likewise, setting the mind upon self, the world, or the desires of the sinful nature will produce selfish, worldly, and sinful thoughts. In contrast, the mind that is set upon the things of the Spirit will be motivated and influenced by the Holy Spirit. *This truth is the most important practical advice for being led by the Spirit.* Learning this principle literally changed the manner in which I made decisions.

Test this out. If you are contemplating a decision, no matter what that decision might be, take some time right now to be filled with the Spirit. Direct your mind to the Lord in prayer and praise. Speak to yourself some great Bible verses. Sing a line or two from a hymn or chorus of praise. Then assess your thoughts. What are you thinking, and how are you feeling about your decision? Assess your thoughts at other times—perhaps when you are at work, caught in a traffic jam, watching television, or filled with self. You will find that your feelings, thoughts, impressions, and desires will flip-flop at different times throughout the day.

As you learn to set your mind upon the things of the Spirit and put the desires of the old sinful nature to death, your mind is being renewed. As a result, by testing and examining what is going on within you, you are learning to discern the will of God.

## Reason and Senses

Recently I was speaking with a theologically astute member of the clergy who was not open to the idea of letting the Holy Spirit lead and direct our thoughts. He said, "God has given us the ability to reason and use common sense. We should use those in our decision making. If we happen to make the wrong decision, then we can always run to the cross of Jesus Christ and receive our forgiveness."

There is no doubt that God has given us our reasoning capabilities and common sense. But reasoning and common sense are also able to be influenced by the devil, the world, and our old sinful nature. The issue is not whether or not we should use our reasoning and common sense, nor whether or not we are forgiven if we make wrong decisions. The issue is this: Before using our reasoning and common sense, should we not first be filled with the Spirit by directing our hearts and minds to God's Word and singing choruses and hymns of praise? Our reasoning and common sense are affected by whether we are filled with self or the Spirit. Clearly, then, we want to be filled with the Spirit and set our minds on the things of the Spirit before we use our reasoning and common sense!

## From Principle to Practice

Some years ago I was offered the opportunity to move to another part of the country. I wanted to move, and I thought the Lord was telling us to move. My wife didn't. As is often the case (and I hate to say it), she was right.

The whole time that I thought about whether or not to accept this opportunity to move, there was an interesting flip-flopping dynamic going on within my reasoning and common sense. When I was in a bad mood, filled with self, and having a pity party, my attitude was, "Let's get out of here! Let's move. I'm sick and tired of this place." But when my thoughts were influenced by the Holy Spirit—when I was praying, leading worship, praising and thanking God—my attitude changed in the opposite direction: "Your ministry is not finished here. Don't move. It is not the will of God."

Finally, when the time came for me to respond to those who had offered me the opportunity to move, I said, "No, it seems good to my wife and the Holy Spirit that I stay where I am at."

The process I just described is, as far as I can tell, exactly what Paul was teaching in Romans 12:2. Having your mind renewed by the Holy Spirit enables you to examine the situation and discern what is the will of God.

## Separating the Spirit from Business Matters

All too often, within the local church or in Christian ministries, people who are involved in decision making end up separating their devotional or spiritual life from the mundane "business" tasks. Meetings or conventions are often opened with a time of prayer and worship which, in the minds of the participants, is to be kept separate from the actual business at hand.

I wonder what would happen in these meetings if the practice of being filled with the Spirit became not only an opening procedure but a part of the entire agenda. Before making any decisions, the participants would be encouraged to set their minds on the things of the Spirit and sing hymns, psalms, and spiritual songs, and then proceed to vote. I wonder if that would make a difference? I think it would.

When the first church convention was held in Jerusalem (Acts 15), the purpose of the meeting was to determine how to handle the participation of Gentile believers in what had been a predominantly Jewish church. Eventually a decision was made, and it's interesting to note the reasoning behind the decision. The apostles wrote, "It seemed good to the Holy Spirit and to us not to burden you"(verse 28). I wonder how many people can say after church meetings, "It seemed good to the Holy Spirit and to us."

I knew a pastor whose church was famous for having long, knock-down, drag-out business meetings. The people would spend hours battling over any issue. Arguments ensued. Hard feelings and contention resulted.

The pastor knew these meetings needed to change, and he decided to try something new. With the approval of his elders, he gathered the entire assembly in the sanctuary to sing hymns, hear the Word of God, and receive the Lord's Supper before the meeting began. This added over 30 minutes to the beginning of the meeting, but it also subtracted more than an hour from the length of the meeting itself. When the people in the church were focused upon the Spirit, their fleshly, argumentative, contentious attitudes were put to rest. Minds were changed. Isn't that great?

## Having Your Mind Changed

Scripture constantly reminds us that many of the great heroes of the faith were not eager to do the will of God. They had to have their minds changed. For example, Noah did not want to build a boat in his backyard. Moses wanted to tend sheep and not confront the Pharaoh of Egypt. The whole nation of Israel chose the wilderness instead of fighting giants. Gideon was not thrilled with the notion of taking on the Midianites. Jonah did not jump for joy when the Lord told him to go to Nineveh. Isaiah argued over whether or not he was God's prophet. And in the New Testament, Peter balked at the idea of embracing Gentile converts. He had to be convinced.

Even today, there are Christians (ourselves included) who are hesitant to do God's will. While his will is always best for us, it may not be what we want at the moment.

I have observed, after being a pastor for 30 years, that church members who are determining to act contrary to the will of God or who are living in sin will often avoid coming to church. Why? When they gather together with God's people, hear God's Word, and sing hymns of praise and thanksgiving, they sense the Spirit speaking to their hearts about God's will or they are convicted of their sin. They don't want that!

Some time ago one member of my congregation was contemplating divorcing his wife. For a long time he avoided coming to worship. We talked about it. I did not, by using the law, attempt to change his mind. I simply said, "All I am asking you to do is come to church, hear the Word of God, and join us for the Lord's table."

After some argument, he agreed to those terms. Later on he changed his mind about the divorce!

Perhaps, rather than providing support groups for divorced singles, God's people might be better served if the church offered classes on teaching married couples how to be filled with the Spirit, have their minds renewed, and learn the process of discerning the will of God.

## "But I am Always Right!"

Many of us, myself included, do not like the idea of having our mind changed. Because of the sinful nature, we are stubborn, adamant, contentious, and think we are always right. We want our way!

Yet some of us have learned from experience that the problems we have often result from insisting on our own way. If you are not willing to have your mind renewed and possibly changed, you will not be able to be led by the Spirit. And that could lead to problems.

One evening a young woman asked me to meet with her and her husband. When we got together, he made it obvious that he did not want to be there. She explained that he had met another woman and was beginning to file for divorce. She did not want the divorce.

I asked him, "Are you willing to have your mind changed about this divorce?"

"No!" he said adamantly. "I want out. I have made up my mind."

"Are you willing to be made willing?" I asked. If he was, I could have led the couple in a Bible study or spent time with them in prayer so that the Holy Spirit could be given an opportunity to work on his will. I knew of other situations where the Lord had intervened, and my hope was to ask God to work on this husband and change his mind.

"No!" he responded angrily. "I already told you that my mind is made up."

"There is nothing I can do," I said somewhat sadly to the wife. "And, as far as I can tell, there is nothing you can do either."

The man got his divorce. With his attitude I would not be at all surprised if by now he has gone through two or three more divorces.

## Presenting Ourselves to God

In Romans 12:1, Paul urges us to present ourselves to God because of the mercy that God has shown us in Christ Jesus. Paul then defines that presentation of ourselves to God as our "spiritual act of worship." The Greek word for "spiritual" is not the typical word *pneumatikos*, but is the word *logikos*. The latter word was made popular by Aristotle and other Greek philosophers. Strictly speaking, it means "logical." In the KJV, the word *logikos* was translated "reasonable."

Paul was saying that since Jesus gave himself for us to forgive and redeem us, it is logical or reasonable for us to present ourselves to him. That is our worship.

Some years ago I talked about Romans 12:1 in a Bible class that was studying the topic of yielding ourselves to God. A young woman came up to me after class and sadly confessed, "I am afraid to give myself to God. I am afraid of what he might expect of me. I am afraid of what I might become."

I suspect there are many Christians who, if pressed, would echo the sentiments shared by this young woman. We are afraid to give over the control of our life to another, even if that other is our Father in heaven, who was willing to let his only Son die for us. We want to remain in control.

Yet once you cross that line and are willing to declare, "Lord, here I am. Have your way with me," you'll finally discover true freedom. And you'll discover something more: God is more interested in your happiness, well-being, and meaning and purpose in life than you are.

Indeed, because of what God has done for you, it is logical and reasonable for you to present yourself unto God!

Do not be conformed to the thinking of this world.

Be transformed as the Holy Spirit renews your mind.

Then you will be able to discern and discover the good, pleasing, and perfect will of God.

If the devil, the world, and our old sinful
nature are able to affect the way that we think,
should we not grant the same ability to
to the Holy Spirit who dwells within us?

# 9

# How the Spirit Leads Us

When we are filled with the Spirit and our minds are renewed by the Spirit, we will respond to challenges and opportunities in a different way. Perhaps the Spirit will lead us to change our mind. Or maybe we will come up with ideas that seem to be leading us in a specific direction.

The Bible clearly illustrates that the Holy Spirit does provide specific direction at times. He told Philip to draw near to the chariot of the Ethiopian (Acts 8:29). He hindered the apostolic team from entering into Asia and Bithynia (Acts 16:7). In a dream, he led them to go to Europe (Acts 16:9). The people of Judah came to the prophet Jeremiah and asked, "Pray that the LORD your God will tell us where we should go and what we should do" (Jeremiah 42:3). Nehemiah spoke of what God had put into his heart to do for Jerusalem (Nehemiah 2:12).

It is one thing to have the Holy Spirit influence a decision that we are facing. But it is a different and far more intriguing matter to have the Spirit direct us to follow a certain path or begin a specific work. This can be exciting, but also somewhat precarious.

## The Origin of Good Ideas

Every innovative, unique, successful work ever established began with a good idea. That is true in both the secular and the religious context. Ford sells automobiles by claiming that they have "a better idea."

Ministries in the church also begin with ideas. There are no exceptions. Nothing happens by itself. The Evangelism Explosion program developed by D. James Kennedy, Robertson's 700 Club, and Christian Research Institute all began with an idea or a concept. Think of some of the popular movements today: Church Growth, Promise Keepers, Concerts of Prayers, Holy Laughter, True Love Waits, Christians United for Reformation, and the Christian Coalition all began with an idea that entered into the mind of the founder of the movement or ministry.

Are there different sources for our ideas? Certainly! The devil, the world, and our old sinful flesh can be rather innovative. The author of the popular book *A Course in Miracles* claims that the ideas in the book were transmitted by a spirit-guide. Can the Holy Spirit give us good ideas? Of course he can!

## The Danger of a Passive Mind

Before we talk more about ideas from the Spirit, I want to address a concern about the condition of the mind into which the Holy Spirit may inject thoughts or impressions. Even though at this point I do not want to spend a great deal of time on this subject, what I'm about to say must be said to avoid confusion.

There are many people who seek the guidance of the Spirit by first establishing a blank, passive mind. Or they attempt to enter an altered state of consciousness as a necessary "pre-condition" for receiving ideas and impressions. J. I. Packer comments:

> Some seek guidance by making their minds blank and receiving what then rises into consciousness as divine directive. This was a daily devotional routing in Frank Buchman's Oxford Group (afterwards Moral Rearmament). . . . Those who assume that whatever "vision" fills the blank is from God have no defense against the invasion of obsessive, grandiose, self-serving imaginations spawned by their own conceit.[1]

I would take the warning a step further. It is a fact that the passive mind or an unthinking altered state of consciousness is the condition required in most occult activities. A vacant mind may well draw some kind of a spiritual invasion, but it is not an invasion from the Holy Spirit.

The Bible is clear. Our minds are to be set on the things of the Holy Spirit. Filled with the Word of God. Overflowing with praise and thanksgiving. Occupied with thoughts of God's greatness and glory. It is in this mental condition that Holy Spirit works.

## Good Advice About Ideas

Some years ago while I was serving a parish in Michigan, a British evangelist spoke at our weekly Prayer and Praise gathering. He taught on the subject of how the Holy Spirit leads and directs. He asked, "If your mind is focused upon the things of this world, and you get an idea, might it be true that the idea will be worldly?"

We all nodded in agreement. Then he asked, "If your mind is obsessed with the offerings of your sinful nature,

and you get an idea, might it be true that the idea origi-
nated in the sinful flesh? Or, if your mind is engaged in
using occult techniques, and you get an idea or a flash of
insight, might it be true that the idea or insight has a de-
monic origin?"

Again, we all nodded in agreement.

"But," he went on, "if your mind is focused on the
Lord, and you are seeking and worshiping Jesus, and
you get an idea or a flash of insight, might it be the
Holy Spirit?"

*Sounds reasonable,* I thought to myself. *If our
thoughts can be prompted by the devil, the world, and our
old sinful nature, why can't they also be prompted by the
Holy Spirit?*

The evangelist went on to demonstrate that what he
was teaching was clearly taught in the Bible. He pointed
out that in Romans 8:5-6, the apostle Paul taught us to
set our minds upon the things of the Spirit so that we
will walk in the Spirit and will be led by the Spirit.

## Putting It Into Practice

The next morning I drove to town to visit some church
members who were in the hospital. I had the
opportunity to put into practice what I had learned the
night before. As was often the case, I used the time in
the car to do some thinking and praying. Praise music
was on the car radio.

On the way to the hospital, I passed by a local television station that had a high tower reaching into the
heavens. As I drove by, I got a strange idea: "Go in there
and tell them you want to start a Bible teaching program
on television."

"That's a dumb idea," I thought to myself with a little giggle. "All I know about television is how to turn on the set." I drove past the building.

A few hundred yards down the road, I thought to myself, *Maybe that was the Holy Spirit telling me to do that.*

I pulled over to the side of the road, stopped the car, and got into an interesting two-sided argument with myself. *It would be stupid for me to go into that station and tell them to put me on television. They would think I was an idiot.* But the other side argued, *What do you care what people think? What do you have to lose? They don't know you from a hole in the ground.*

So I started the car, turned around, and drove back to the television station. I won't go into all the details of what happened, but, in a nutshell, I talked to the program director, who was a Christian. He offered me the opportunity to do a half-hour demonstration tape just to see if I had the ability to present myself on television. That evening, I met with the elders at our church. I told them what I had done, and mentioned the offer to do the demonstration tape. They supported the opportunity, affirmed it, and financially backed it. Some "major money" people heard about the project and were interested in getting involved. The new pastor at a neighboring congregation, who had a degree in radio and television, heard about my endeavor and presented his services. I got hooked up with a syndicating distribution agency. We heard about an organization that was interested in providing programming for cable-origination channels. At the time, cable television was in its infancy. In six months, I was doing a 30-minute Bible study program on three commercial channels and many cable stations around on the country.

All that took place 25 years ago. I taught on television for two years. The TV ministry served as a catalyst that developed a praise choir that performed concerts far and wide. I started a newsletter that became a small magazine. We also started a fully equipped print shop and opened a Christian book store. Some of the articles I wrote for the magazine contributed toward my first book on inner healing.

Now, 25 years later, after many changes, adjustments, and moves to different parts of the country, I host a two-hour network radio talk show called "Issues, etc." And I have written four books (including this one).

All of these ministries are interconnected and came about as a result of following the initial prompting to start a television ministry. While it is not possible to look ahead and perceive the hand of God in all the details of our lives, from my perspective today as I review the last 25 years, the willingness to follow what I perceived to be a silly idea about starting a television ministry was the defining moment of my ministry.

## What About Mundane Matters?

The New Testament clearly affirms that the Holy Spirit can and does direct our thoughts and decisions. The process involves being filled with the Spirit and having our minds renewed by the Spirit.

But how far do you take the practice of following the thoughts, ideas, and impressions that you believe are from the Spirit?

In a cassette-tape message by a fairly well-known Bible teacher, I heard a story about how he allowed himself to be led by the Spirit while he was in the woods picking blackberries. As he wandered through the woods, he prayed and hummed songs of praise. Whenever a thought entered his mind about which path he should take in his search for blackberries, he followed the thought. He claimed that as a result, he found some choice blackberry bushes hidden in the brush—which he would not have discovered unless he followed what he perceived to be the leading of the Holy Spirit. He then said that following the leading of the Holy Spirit was a process to be learned, and the best way to learn it was through mundane matters—such as picking blackberries.

Some authors who have written about seeking the will of God or being led by the Spirit are often critical of those who claim to be led by the Spirit in nonspiritual matters such as shopping, deciding what to wear, trading in a car or, for that matter, picking blackberries.

I do not agree with that criticism. I believe that being led by the Holy Spirit is a process to be learned. Some years ago when I was learning the process, I would go into the church office in the morning, be filled with the Spirit by getting into the Word and through prayer and praise, and then ask, "Lord, what do you want me to do first?" Some task would come to mind (usually something that I did not want to do). After I completed that task, I would follow the next thought. Using that process, I was amazed at the amount of meaningful work I would complete in the course of a day. If you are a housewife who is at home all day and you try the process, don't be surprised if you sense the Spirit saying, "Make the beds" or, "Do the dishes."

Some Christians today consider themselves too so-phisticated to even entertain the notion of being led by the Holy Spirit. They might readily dismiss some of the things that I have been sharing with you and categorize them as silliness. I wonder how they would have re-sponded to some of Jesus' directives? Would they have also dismissed them as silliness?

For example, how would you have responded if Jesus looked at you and said, "Here is what I want you to do. Get your fishing pole and go down to the lake. Bait your hook and throw the line in the water. After you catch the first fish, open its mouth, and inside you will find a coin. Use that coin to pay our temple tax."

Can you imagine how some Christians today would have responded to those instructions? They would say, "That's silly!" But that is what Jesus told Peter to do (Matthew 17:24-27). Imagine Peter going home and grabbing his fishing pole. His wife asks, "Peter, where are you going?" Would Peter have had the nerve to say, "I'm going fishing to pay for the temple tax"? What was Peter thinking when he baited his hook, tossed the line in the water, and waited for the first fish to bite? I know what I would have thought: "Lord, this is ridiculous!"

I do not want to criticize people who say that they fol-low the Spirit's leading in mundane matters, but I would offer a suggestion: Don't tell anybody what you are doing or the results of what you are doing. Keep this between you and the Lord. (If you get together with other Christians and announce that the Spirit led you to put on a specific outfit or to wear a certain tie, someone in the group might question the Holy Spirit's taste in clothing.)

We shouldn't be afraid to be childlike when we at-tempt to discern the Spirit's leading. When we are learn-ing doctrine or studying theology, by all means we should be careful to examine the facts and use our in-tellects. That is God's will for us. But when it comes to personal piety, living in relationship with our Father in heaven, or seeking to be led by the Holy Spirit, we should be childlike. Being childlike is living in truth be-cause it corresponds with Scripture's description of the kind of relationship we have with God.

## Exercising Caution

God has given his Word to us and has clearly stated that certain behavior and practices are inherently wrong, and it is impossible for the Holy Spirit to lead us *contrary* to God's revealed Word. I read about a woman who took some money her boss had left on his desk. She said she got the impression that what she did was right because the Bible says, "All things are yours" (1 Corinthians 3:21). But the Holy Spirit would not lead a person contrary to the commandment, "Don't steal." Nor could I say, for ex-ample, "I got an impression from the Holy Spirit that I am to leave my wife and marry another woman." Why not? The Bible says that to do so is wrong.

There are people who have discontinued taking vital medication because they believed that was what the Spirit told them to do. But it's foolish to put your life at stake simply because you *perceived* some kind of leading from the Holy Spirit. I am always willing to stake my life on the validity of God's promises as revealed in the Bible, but I would never stake my life on a mere subjec-tive impression.

Receiving thoughts or subjective impressions that you believe are from the Holy Spirit and acting on those ideas can produce a rather exciting Christian lifestyle. You may step out in a direction, initiate a specific ministry, or go out and pick blackberries. Now I am not so foolish as to suggest that these ideas and impressions are definitely from the Holy Spirit. Discernment is always essential.

If you come up with an idea that includes other people, involves a risk for you or your family, demands a major financial investment, or will radically change the direction of your life, be careful! I agree with the wisdom of J. I. Packer when he writes:

> My point is not that the Spirit of God gives no impressions, but rather that impressions must be rigorously tested by biblical wisdom—the corporate wisdom of the believing community as well as personal wisdom. . . . People who receive impressions about what they should believe or do should question such impressions until they have been thoroughly tested.[2]

## The Holy Spirit Knows What He is Doing

One of the young men from a church I served in Michigan went to a Christian college in California. One day after chapel was over, he caught the eye of young woman a few rows in front of him. As he was looking at her, he got the impression, "You are going to marry this girl." He then went over to her and invited her to go out and get a cup of coffee that evening. She very readily agreed.

As they were sitting in the restaurant, being a gutsy kind of guy, he told her that when he saw her after chapel that he sensed the Lord telling him that they would get married one day. Amazingly, she said that the same idea had crossed her mind when she saw him. (I'm not making this up!)

Well, after nine months of courtship, meeting each other's families, and speaking with their college counselors, they got engaged and set a date. That next summer, I drove to California with my family and conducted the ceremony.

Obviously, this is not a normal way to find a wife or a husband, but it did happen. Fortunately, they took the time to give their impressions a thorough examination. They would have been foolish to hop in a car on the night that they met and drive to Reno to get married. While they believed their impressions were from the Holy Spirit, they also believed that God required those impressions to be rigorously tested. They were not doing something mundane, like picking blackberries.

Nearly 25 years have passed since that happened. From what I understand, they are a great Christian couple with a wonderful family. They have experienced some heartaches over health problems, but their relationship has remained solid.

Receiving ideas and impressions that you believe are from the Holy Spirit is only one element in the dimension of divine guidance. It is only the initial step in a process. There is far more involved, as we'll see in the upcoming chapters.

Since the Holy Spirit is the Divine Director of the Body of Christ, being led by the Spirit will produce divinely orchestrated circumstances.

**10**

# Using Discernment

Let's say that you have come up with an idea or an impression that you believe is from the Holy Spirit. Perhaps it entails the beginning of a ministry of some kind or another, or starting a small business on the side, or pursuing a different career, or sharing your faith with a fellow worker. Once the idea or impression is in place, how do you proceed?

In earlier chapters, we learned that being led by the Holy Spirit is a process. In Romans 12:2 the apostle Paul spoke about the renewed mind "proving what is the will of God." The Greek word he used for "prove" means to examine by testing.

## Examining the Circumstances

When you attempt to discern the leading of the Holy Spirit, it is important—in addition to testing your thoughts, desires, and impressions—to examine the circumstances. A "circumstance" is that which is happening around you while you are standing. While the Holy Spirit dwells in you personally and can influence your thoughts, insights, and decisions, he also works behind the scenes. He sets the stage. He confirms or negates your decisions with circumstances.

In Ephesians 2:10 we read, "We are God's workmanship, created in Christ Jesus to do good works, which God *prepared in advance* for us to do" (emphasis added). That is a great truth. As God's people, we can believe that God has prepared things for us to do. Our task is to simply discover and walk in those things.

Consider the story I shared with you in the previous chapter—when I was led by the Holy Spirit to begin a television ministry. As I see it, the Holy Spirit knew that on a particular day I would hear someone teach about being led by the Holy Spirit. The Spirit also knew that the next day, I would be driving into the city and passing the television station. He knew that the program director was one of his children. He knew that there was another pastor in my community who had media experience. So all he had to do was tap me on the shoulder and ask me to walk in what he had already prepared.

I once heard a Bible teacher say, "If the idea crosses your mind that you are to become a missionary to India, and you think it might be the Holy Spirit, don't sell your home and move to India just because of the idea. But, if the idea comes to mind and shortly afterward you get a letter with a $10,000 check enclosed encouraging you to become a missionary to India, you should begin packing."

## The Holy Spirit Hinders

I have often wondered about the time when the Holy Spirit forbade the apostles from going in specific directions (Acts 16:6-7). I wonder how he did that? We read in Acts 16:6-7:

> Paul and his companions traveled throughout the region of Phyrgia and Galatia, having been kept by the Holy Spirit from preaching the word in the province of Asia. When they came to the border of Mysia, they tried to enter Bithynia, but the Spirit of Jesus would not allow them to.

How did the Spirit keep the apostles from preaching in Asia? And how were they hindered from entering Bithynia even though they attempted to enter? There had to be circumstances involved. Perhaps the apostles came to the border of Asia and Timothy became ill, and Paul and Barnabas got into a heated argument. Perhaps the three of them had a hard time sleeping at night. As they reviewed the situation at breakfast the next morning, they arrived at the conclusion that the Holy Spirit was hindering them from going to Asia. That may have also happened when they got to Bithynia. They tried to enter, but the Spirit of Jesus somehow stopped them from doing it.

The account in Acts 16 brings us back to the issues of *how* and *when*. Because Jesus told his disciples to preach the Gospel throughout the world, we know it was his will that the Gospel should also be preached in Asia and Bithynia. But, as far as the Holy Spirit was concerned, the time was not right. So he stopped them.

## The Spirit Persuades

During his early ministry, the apostle Peter had some negative feelings toward Gentiles. He was a committed member of the household of Israel. To him, Gentiles were unclean. He had no desire to preach the Gospel to the Gentiles until the Holy Spirit strongly persuaded him to do so. When you read the story of Peter and Cornelius recorded in Acts chapter 10, you can see how beautifully the Holy Spirit set Peter up for the task that he had prepared for Peter to walk into.

An angel appears to Cornelius and tells the soldier to send for Peter. Cornelius sends three men to Peter's house. Peter is at home on the roof of his house waiting for lunch to be prepared. He has a vision of a sheet coming down from heaven. This sheet is filled with unclean animals. A voice says, "Kill and eat." Peter says, "No Lord, these animals are unclean." The voice says, "Do not call unclean what I have made clean." The vision is repeated two more times. When Peter comes to his senses and thinks about what he saw, the Spirit gives him the impresssion that there are three men knocking on the door looking for him. The Spirit says, "Get up and go with them." He obeys. He goes to Cornelius' house and preaches the Gospel. As a result, the first group of Gentiles, considered unclean by the Jews, were converted.

Peter's actions opened him to criticism from his fellow Jews because Gentiles were supposedly unclean. Do you think Peter could have convinced them that it was the Holy Spirit who had persuaded him to do what he did?

## The Interaction of the Body of Christ

Sometimes the Holy Spirit will set up circumstances in a way that leads other people to do something in conjunction with what he is leading you to do. The Holy Spirit is the Divine Director of the Body of Christ. He can bring different people together to accomplish a common goal. Some of the ways he does this can be amazing.

While I was living in Michigan, I was invited to come to New York City, my hometown, and speak at a conference. As I crossed the George Washington Bridge and viewed the majestic skyline of the Big Apple, a very clear thought or impression entered my mind: "You will be moving back to New York."

At that time, I had been in Michigan for over 10 years, and it seemed to me that it was time to move on. So when I got back home after the conference, I told my wife, Dianne, what I was thinking. She had no objection.

Some days later, I decided to sit down and write a letter to my denomination's district superintendent over the area that included New York City. I had known the man from my college years. I was simply going to inform him that I was available and ask him to keep me in mind if there were any parishes in that area looking for a pastor. For some reason, I was having difficulty putting my thoughts on paper. Then the thought entered my mind, *Why don't you just call his office?*

So I looked up his phone number and, just as I went into my office and reached for the telephone, it rang. I picked up the phone, greeted the caller, and heard a familiar voice saying, "Matzat, we would like to open up some doors for you to move to New York. Would you be interested?"

The voice on the other end belonged to my former pastor, who at the moment happened to be in the district superintendent's office. They had heard from a third party that I was interested in moving to New York. Amazingly, I had just been getting ready to call the same phone from which he was calling me.

I was stunned by this unexpected surprise! After telling my former pastor that I was definitely interested, I immediately called Dianne, who was having lunch with a friend at a local restaurant. I told her, "I am quite certain I know where we will be moving." About four months later we left Michigan and moved to New York City.

Was this a mere coincidence? I think not. For me, it was a circumstance based upon the the Holy Spirit's working within the Body of Christ. The Holy Spirit had led the pastor in New York to call me from superintendent's office at the exact time that I was getting ready to call the same office. The circumstance confirmed what I believed to be an impression from the Holy Spirit that we would be moving to New York.

## Lord, Please Bail Us Out

In the Greek text of the New Testament, the Holy Spirit is called the *paraclete*, or "one who is called alongside to help." In our desire to be led by the Spirit, there will be times when we make mistakes. And because the Holy Spirit is our helper, he is always there for us, ready to help us get out of a bad situation.

During the time that I was involved in television ministry, we opened a Christian bookstore. We had two volunteers who ordered the materials. On one occasion a certain Christian supplier talked them into ordering more material than we had resources. They ordered us $1,500 dollars into debt. As the weeks passed, the supplier demanded his money, which we did not have. My prayer was, "Lord, please bail us out." Amazingly, I was not distressed. All along I felt the Holy Spirit was saying, "I will take care of it."

Some days later I was invited to lead a Bible study in a church about 50 miles away. After the gathering was over, a young man who was familiar with our television and publishing ministry came up to me and asked, "Are you having financial difficulties?"

"Funny you should ask," I replied. "Yes, we are."

"Well," he went on to explain. "I had a dream last night that you were having financial problems and that I helped you out. I believe this could be the Holy Spirit. Here is a check."

I almost fell over when I looked at it. It was for $1,500.

Was this the work of the Holy Spirit or just a coincidence? I believe it was the Holy Spirit—the Divine Director of the Body of Christ.

## A Fish Story

The Holy Spirit is not just involved in ministry-related activities. He can also lead us and set the stage in our business dealings.

Tom, a good friend of mine and a committed Christian, owns a deli in Manhattan. In his business, he uses a great deal of tuna for salads and sandwiches. Before he became a Christian, he was getting his tuna in huge quantities at highly cut-rate prices from a questionable source, if you know what I mean.

After Tom became a Christian, the Holy Spirit seemed to be convicting him about buying the tuna from a questionable supplier. He no longer felt right about it, but he was also was apprehensive about getting out of the deal. He was a bit nervous about the prospect of having his legs broken.

We talked about it, and Tom decided to trust the Lord. I encouraged him to tell Louie "the tuna dealer" the truth, and we committed the situation to the Lord.

Well, a few days later, Louie came into the store to take the next month's order of tuna.

"Louie," Tom said while biting his lip, "I can't take anymore of your tuna. I have become a Christian, and I believe the Holy Spirit is telling me that buying this tuna from you is not right."

Louie threw up his arms in despair. "Not you, too!" he exclaimed. "My wife has also become some kind of a born-again Christian, and she keeps telling me that what I am doing is not right."

He turned around and walked out of the store, never to be heard from again.

The fact that Louie's wife was a Christian helped to create a circumstance that allowed Tom to peacefully back out of a bad situation. In addition, Tom provided for Louie's wife a confirming testimony of her witness to her husband. I wouldn't be surprised if by now Louie was a Christian. If that were the case, to what might he attribute it? Possibly the witness that he received from both his wife and Tom.

## Those "Fish People"

There are Christians today who believe that the Spirit can bring different believers together to achieve a common goal, but sometimes they apply the dynamic in the wrong situations.

There was a Christian man who felt that the Lord wanted him to buy a different car. While at one particular used-car lot he met a saleman who was also Christian. He interpreted this chance encounter with a fellow believer to be a divinely ordained circumstance confirming his desire for a different car. He made a purchase and later discovered that he had been ripped off.

There are many businesses today that display the "fish" or ixthus symbol. *Ixthus* is an acrostic for the Greek words that spell "Jesus Christ, God's Son, Savior." It was the cryptic means used by the early persecuted Christians for identifying one another as believers. Today, the symbol is often used by business owners who profess to be Christians. There are even some communities that publish a "yellow pages" of Christian businesses.

Just because a proprietor displays the fish symbol or claims to be a Christian does not mean that you will, as a result of the Holy Spirit working in his heart, get a better deal. We have a television and appliance dealer in our town who advertises that he is closed on Sundays "in honor of the Lord's day." Does this mean that he will give me, a fellow Christian, a better deal than an unbeliever who is open on Sundays? Not necessarily so.

Finding a proprietor who says he is a Christian is not necessarily a Spirit-led circumstance. In fact, a few businesses may display the fish symbol just to draw naive Christians into their net or to hook them on a bad deal.

On my daily radio talk show we were discussing the growing popularity of businesses that display the fish symbol. One woman called in and complained about, as she put it, "those fish people." It seems she hired some "fish people" to put new siding on her house. They ripped her off both in terms of price and quality. She said, "I will never again trust any of those 'fish people.'"

I personally do not like the idea of Christians identifying themselves as such in order to gain the business of fellow Christians. If a Christian businessman wants to profess his faith in Jesus, I think he should do so through honest dealings and quality work, not by putting a fish symbol on his business card.

## Spirit-led Interaction

Jesus told his disciples that it was for their good that he go away and send the Holy Spirit to guide and help them (John 16:7). This applies to us today as well. When you see the Holy Spirit leading and directing different members of the Body of Christ to interact with one another, led by the Spirit, you can understand what Jesus was talking about. Through the Spirit's guidance, we are able to proclaim the Gospel and enlarge the kingdom of God more effectively than if Jesus had remained on this earth. As you submit yourself to the Spirit's leading in your church, ministry, and personal life, you will be amazed by some of the circumstances that he brings about in order to accomplish his work.

All of this brings us now to an important question. When a fellow Christian, led by the Holy Spirit, provides a circumstance that confirms one of your insights, ideas, or impressions, you may feel blessed to be a part of the church, the Body of Christ. You can see the Holy Spirit at work in both of your lives. But what should you do if a fellow Christian gives you advice contrary to your insights, ideas, or impressions? Are you open to the possibility that the Holy Spirit may try to speak to you through fellow believers and let you know when you have wrongly assumed an idea came from the Spirit?

The Holy Spirit will often lead us
through the advice given by other people.
The question is, are we
willing to listen?

II

# Listening to Other People

Probably the least popular form of guidance is seeking the advice of other Christians. That can be a humbling experience—especially if other believers disagree with what we think is specific direction from the Lord.

This presents us with a catch-22. If we are not willing to seek the advice of others because we are proud, that is a good indicator that our ideas and impressions are coming from our stubborn, sinful nature rather than from the Holy Spirit. In Ephesians 5:21, the apostle Paul defines one of the elements of living the Spirit-filled life as submitting ourselves "to one another out of reverence for Christ." So we are "stuck." If we do seek the advice of others, we take the risk that they may tell us we are wrong. If we are not willing to submit and seek the advice of others out of reverence for Christ, then chances are that we are already wrong.

Since we are a part of the church, which is defined as the Body of Christ, we are members one of another. Therefore, we should learn to depend upon and listen to each other. I like the way Blaine Smith puts it:

> . . . any serious endeavor to know God's will should not be an isolated effort but one shared with other

Christians. If my commitment to Christ is inseparable from my commitment to other believers, then I must not expect to understand his will fully apart from being in relationship with other Christians, and I should expect that he will often convey his will to me through others.[1]

## Confirming Each Other's Mistakes

Of course, there is one way out of the dilemma. We can handpick our advisors. We can choose to seek the counsel of only those who have been known to always agree with us. But that can be destructive.

Read the story of Ahab, King of Israel, and Micaiah the prophet (1 Kings 22:1-28). Ahab had his own band of 400 handpicked prophets who always told him what he wanted to hear. Micaiah was the only faithful prophet in Israel. Ahab hated Micaiah, because he dared to tell the king the truth. As the king was preparing to go to war, only Micaiah had the nerve to predict his defeat and imminent death, but Ahab refused to listen. As it turned out, Ahab died.

Thus, seeking advice from those who always agree with you is not a way out. It is a way into deception and possible destruction.

Ministries that have a nonprofit status and seek tax exemption are required to have a board of directors. If you examine the makeup of the boards of the two leading televangelists who fell into immorality, you discover interesting similarities.

One of the preachers, who seemed to be rather headstrong, had a board composed primarily of family members who probably always agreed with him. After his fall into immorality, the authorities within his denomination, out of genuine concern for his future, told him to get out of the ministry for a time. He refused to listen to them. From his perspective, his fall into sin was not the result of his bad decisions. Rather, the devil made him do it.

The other preacher had a board made up of friends. One of those friends, a leading figure in the scandal who served some prison time because of his role in the fraud, told me in a radio interview that the board members never disagreed with the ideas and visions of the head man.

"After all," as he explained, "look what he had accomplished. Who were we to tell him that he was wrong?" If they would have been willing to tell him the truth, he probably would not have had to spend several years in jail.

Like King Ahab, both men had gathered around them people who would agree with them and confirm their wrong judgments and decisions.

## Seeking Out Your Adversaries

Two of the churches that I served gave the pastor the responsibility of choosing men to serve as elders, rather than letting the congregation elect the elders. The elders' role was to assist in the ministry and to advise the pastor in spiritual matters.

When I chose a man to become an elder, I looked at his spiritual qualifications. Was he faithful in worship? Did he attend Bible classes? Did his life demonstrate the fruit of his faith? In addition, in some cases, I sought out men who were willing to disagree with me. Some of them had strong opinions about some of my policies and practices. On occassion, some men questioned the direction I was leading the congregation.

I remember approaching a certain man, who was a faithful member of the church, and asking him to be an elder. He was somewhat surprised.

"Why do you want me to be an elder?" he asked. There are some issues on which I do not agree with you."

"That's why I want you to be an elder," was my reply. He was somewhat taken back.

This practice produces good results. That's because a person who voices objections in a congregation is looking for a forum in which to be heard. When you place a person in that forum, and you pray together, he begins to realize that his views are being heard. Since his views may influence policy or direction, he suddenly becomes "slow to speak." And ultimately, if you come to an agreement with a person with whom you normally disagree, the chances that you are being led by the Spirit are rather good.

## The Warnings to Paul

There may be times when a person feels strongly about a specific leading of the Holy Spirit and cannot be dissuaded. This, apparently, is what happened at the end of Paul's third missionary journey. He speaks of himself as being "compelled by the Spirit" to go to Jerusalem, yet at every city he visits along the way, he is warned about the imprisonment and hardships that await him (Acts 20:22-23). After leaving Troas and landing at Tyre, he gathered with the disciples in that city. They, too, urged him "through the Spirit" not to go to Jerusalem (Acts 21:4). He went on to Caesarea and met with the disciples living there. The prophet Agabus from Judea came to Caesarea, bound Paul's hands and feet with his own belt, and told Paul that such fate awaited him in Jerusalem. Finally, when Paul would not be dissuaded, the disciples in Caesarea declared, "The Lord's will be done" (Acts 21:14).

It is rather difficult to figure out what was happening in these situations. Was Paul being stubborn and not willing to listen? I have read some authors who felt that Paul had a Christ-complex and wanted to go to Jerusalem, be put to death, and attain to the resurrection from the dead, as Jesus did. I do not agree.

It seems to me that Paul's commitment to go to Jerusalem was so strong—even though there is no evidence to indicate that his decision was confirmed by anyone else—that he would not be dissuaded. When a person acts as Paul did, the only thing you can say to thim is, "May God's will be done."

You might ask, "If Paul could be so stubborn, then why can't I simply do my own thing and forget what other people say?"

The answer is simple: You are not the apostle Paul!

The incident in Acts 20-21 does provide us with this clear teaching: Even though the Holy Spirit wants us to seek the advice and counsel of other Christian brothers and sisters, we are still responsible for our own decisions and behavior. If you *do* listen to someone else and he happens to be wrong, you cannot blame him for it. You must decide whether or not to listen. It is your decision.

## Submitting to Authority

There are some teachings about submission to authority, especially among charismatic Christians, that are wrong and produce bondage. Some people teach that Christians should totally submit themselves to their spiritual shepherds and do whatever they are told to do because that is how the will of God is communicated. Blaine Smith comments on this kind of deception:

> We must conclude that a Christian is not required to regard the counsel of a spiritual leader as the will of God by definition. While we should seek counsel from qualified spiritual leaders in making major personal decisions, we must not feel under any compulsion to regard this counsel uncritically as divine guidance. We may feel free to weigh it along with other factors which appear to be pointing towards God's will.[2]

There is currently a movement among charismatics to go to "prophets" to discover the will of God. A popular craze for some alleged spiritual leaders is to establish "schools of the prophets," where men are taught to speak directive, prophetic words to other Christians. Those who receive these "prophetic words" are expected to regard them as the will of God for their lives. I agree with Mike Moriarty, who speaks about this new prophetic heresy in his book *The New Charismatics*:

> The new charismatic practice of personal prophecy has done much to obscure. . . . the believer's responsibility in determining God's will for their lives. God's plan is not to leave us in the dark until he releases his modern prophets to turn on the lights. God takes the initiative in guiding us. It is his responsibility to lead us.[3]

Both the "submitting to authority" movement and the prophetic movement have a twofold appeal.

First, they appeal to those who love to have control over the lives of other people. To be in a position where you can tell people what to do and how to live is a fleshly power-trip. I have known Christians who act as if they have the "gift of advice" and hunger to get their fingers into the lives and decisions of other Christians.

When I seek advice and counsel for myself, I always avoid those who want power over me or who feel they know exactly what I should do. I suggest the same to you.

Second, the two movements appeal to those who do not want to take responsibility for their own lives or make their own decisions. It is much easier to simply let someone else tell you what to do—especially if you believe that person's claims that his direction for your life is the will of God.

God has not called us to live either way. He has called us to freedom. He has given to us his Word and Spirit to direct our paths. He prepares the good works for us to walk in. While he desires for us to be interrelated with our fellow believers, he also wants us to take responsibility for our own lives and decisions.

## Listening for the Voice of Jesus

I'm sure it was easy for people to listen to advice from Jesus. When I sit down with another Christian and share my heart, my concerns, or my confusion with him, my hope is that when he responds to me I will be able to hear Jesus speaking to me. I don't mean that in the sense that I would give the person's counsel the same weight I would give the words of Jesus in Scripture. Rather, I am saying that I hope the attitude of the person who is advising me reflects the same attitude Jesus had when he gave advice.

There is a man who heads up one of the ministries in my denomination. He is a good friend. When I have questions or concerns, I speak with him. His advice is always wise, gentle, and insightful. On one occasion while we were having coffee together, I mentioned to him, "When you advise me, it is as if I hear Jesus talking to me." That is the kind Christian you should look for when you are seeking advice.

The apostle James clearly defines the wisdom that comes down from above. He writes in James 3:17:

> Wisdom that comes from heaven is first of all pure; then peace-loving, considerate, submissive, full of mercy and good fruit, impartial and sincere.

Note especially the word "submissive." The KJV uses the phrase "easy to be entreated" to describe the "wisdom from above." The Greek word here means "compliant." In other words, the advice is not a hard word but a soft and gentle word. It is not an opinionated word, or a "I'm right and you're wrong" word, but a word spoken in genuine love and concern.

In the corporate world, people who have positions of authority tell you what to do on the basis of power and position. You listen to your boss because he is the boss. He has a position and title. But in the church or in a ministry, the voice of authority is the voice of Jesus being spoken through other people.

If you desire to know the will of God for your life, then you'll find wisdom in sharing your thoughts with other Christians. And when you seek advice, do not gravitate toward those who always agree with you. Be willing to speak with individuals who may correct you, disagree with you, or warn you ... *but who also love you!*

The Holy Spirit works
in our emotions and feelings. Being at peace
about a situation is a key ingredient to
being led by Holy Spirit. In addition, if we feel
pushed into making a decision, we should
back off. God is in no hurry.

# 12

# How Do You Feel About Your Decision?

Human feelings and emotions have received a bad rap by theologically minded pastors and teachers. While there is no doubt that the essence and substance of the Christian faith is based upon the solid objective facts readily drawn from the clear teachings of God's Word, that does not eliminate the role of our emotions and feelings.

Many Christians have erroneously fallen on two sides of the feelings and emotions issue. There are some people who make the mistake of basing their beliefs upon what they feel. They say, "I know that my sins are forgiven because my conscience is clear." In contrast, there are people who make the correct statement, "I know that my sins are forgiven because the Bible says that Jesus died for me," but these same people are not willing to admit that they feel anything.

As we take a closer look at feelings and emotions, keep in mind that they are not the cause of anything, but rather, they are the result. We are not to believe because we feel something. Rather, we will feel something because of what we believe.

## The Spirit and Your Feelings

When you came to faith in Jesus Christ, an internal adjustment took place in your life. The Holy Spirit entered in. You were born again. Your new life in Jesus Christ affects what you believe, how you think, how you live, what you want, and, of course, how you feel. For this reason, if you are being led by the Spirit rather than by the devil, the world, or your sinful nature, you will feel differently.

For us to use subjective feelings to help discern the leading of the Holy Spirit is neither strange nor mystical. And even when we make decisions on the basis of common sense, we still have a tendency to assess our subjective feelings.

For example, I have an old, banged-up, red car with many miles on it. Recently I contemplated getting rid of it and buying a used car that looked nicer. As I went through the decision-making process, I considered basic practical financial issues and the fact that the old car ran great. But there were also subjective issues: Was I *happy* with the old car? Was I *contented* driving it back and forth to work? On both counts, my answer was yes. Therefore, I kept the old clunker.

If we take our feelings into consideration when dealing with common-sense issues, why shouldn't we also do the same when it comes to discerning the leading of the Spirit?

## Let Peace be the Judge

Often you will hear Christians say that they refused to enter into a work or go in a specific direction because they did not feel at peace about the situation. Is that a legitimate means of discernment?

In Colossians 3:15, Paul writes, "Let the peace of Christ rule in your hearts." In that verse, the Greek word for "rule" actually means "to judge" or "to be the umpire."

A look at the surrounding context shows that Paul is describing the Spirit-filled life (Colossians 3:15-17). One of the elements of the fruit of the Spirit is peace (Galatians 5:22). Paul also tells us that the mind that is controlled by the Spirit produces life and peace (Romans 8:6). He tells the Philippians that if they set their minds on good things, the God of peace will be with them (Philippians 4:8-9). Therefore, if our thoughts, intentions, impressions, or ideas are motivated by the Spirit or by our new life in Christ Jesus, we should experience a sense of peace.

When we are faced with making a decision, then, one of the questions we can ask ourselves is, "Do I have peace about it?" As we have seen in the New Testament, peace is an important ingredient in our internal guidance system.

## The Lack of Peace

In the book of Acts there are some instances in which Paul acted on the basis of his subjective feelings.

For example, in Acts 16:16-18, while in the city of Philippi, the apostles were being followed by a young slave girl who was shouting, "These men are servants of the Most High God, who are telling you the way to be saved."

Even though the woman's proclamation was accurate, Paul was troubled by it (verse 18). The Greek word for "troubled" means "to be annoyed or perplexed." We could properly conclude that Paul's peace of mind was being disturbed. He discerned that the woman was demonized, and turned around and cast a demon out of her.

On another occasion Paul encountered favorable circumstances, yet he had no peace or "rest in his spirit" (2 Corinthians 2:13 KJV). Read carefully what he said:

> Now when I went to Troas to preach the gospel of Christ and found that the Lord had opened a door for me, I still had no peace of mind, because I did not find my brother Titus there. So I said good-by to them and went on to Macedonia (2 Corinthians 2:12-13).

The apostle went to Troas expecting to meet Titus, who had been at Corinth. Because Titus was not there, Paul became anxious. Even though the Lord had set before him an open door to preach the Gospel, he didn't go through it because he had no peace of mind. So he left and went to look for Titus.

## Being Led by Peace

After two years of doing a television Bible study program, the time came to prepare for our third season. The door was wide open. The three commercial stations that carried our program wanted us back. In addition, more doors were opening into cable access. I remember very clearly a conversation I had while playing tennis one day with the Methodist pastor who helped me with the production.

"Well, Don," he said. "It is time to get going with 'Bread of Life.' "

"Chuck," I replied, "I don't think I'll do another year of this. I don't know. For some reason I just don't have any peace about it."

Chuck was not happy with my response, but I didn't feel at peace about continuing the program. I shared my

feelings with the people on the board that had come together to undergird the ministry and they agreed. We
discontinued television and focused our attention onto
printing and publishing.

I have often reflected back on my decision to leave
the television ministry. Perhaps if I had continued, I
could have become a powerful, nationally renowned
televangelist. But then again, I might have also fallen
into sin and been disgraced. Who knows?

I do know one thing: I was at peace with my decision, and being at peace is an important part of seeking
to be led by the Spirit.

## Not the Author of Confusion

While a sense of peace might help us to know if we
should move ahead in a specific direction, the absence
of peace or the presence of confusion might serve as an
indication that we should not get involved in a particular situation.

In 1 Corinthians 14:33, when Paul was addressing
the problems that surfaced during the worship services
in the church at Corinth, he said, "God is not a God of
disorder but of peace." The KJV says that God is not the
author of confusion.

The church at Corinth desired to exercise the gifts
and manifestations of the Holy Spirit. But there was
much confusion during the church services, and Paul
was telling them that was evidence that the Holy Spirit
was not in control. Even though the Corinthian
Christians boasted that they were spiritual, the de-
meanor of their interaction demonstrated otherwise.

Many years ago I was invited to participate in the
local branch of a ministry that placed racks of Christian

books in grocery stores. After sitting through a chaotic meeting attended by the regional salespeople, my response was, "There is no way that I would get involved in this!" The entire operation was in a state of confusion. If this had merely been a worldly, secular business where profit and competition was the only motive, the attitudes of the salespeople would have been normal. But this was supposed to be a ministry. Because it was being operated strictly as a business with profit being the bottom line, I wanted no part.

Now, it's virtually impossible for us to avoid every single situation in which we find chaos and confusion. After all, where would we go? In a world motivated by greed, envy, and the profit motive, confusion resulting from animosity, bitterness, and broken relationships is rampant.

But what about the decisions that we make regarding our involvement in a church or a ministry? I believe we should exercise caution if we see a lack of peace among the people.

When James defined *un*spiritual wisdom, he wrote this:

> If you harbor bitter envy and selfish ambition in your hearts, do not boast about it or deny the truth. Such "wisdom" does not come down from heaven but is earthly, unspiritual, of the devil. For where you have envy and selfish ambition, there you find disorder and every evil practice (James 3:14-16).

If you are searching for a church to join, make sure you don't do not assess the spiritual life of a fellowship only by what you see on a Sunday morning. Rather, attend some of the business meetings and watch how the people interact. Attend a church picnic, or volunteer to serve on a committee. That's where you will see the real life of the congregation.

Of course, no church is perfect, and Christians do make sinful choices at times. We're likely to see that no matter where we go. But confusion should not be the rule in the affairs of a Christian congregation. I have known churches where some of the people actually bragged about the chaotic nature of their business meetings. That is not something to boast of, rather, it is to their shame.

## Pushed or Led?

When you are faced with a decision, before you take a step of faith, I suggest that you ask yourself, "Do I feel pushed or shoved in this direction?" If you feel pushed, I would back off. Remember, God is not in a hurry.

The book of John describes Jesus as the Good Shepherd. It is the task of the shepherd to go before the sheep and lead them. Jesus is not a cowboy who drives—or pushes—cattle. You cannot drive sheep. They scatter. Sheep have to be led. The shepherd has to be very patient.

On one of my trips to Israel, I spent the good part of a Sunday morning sitting on a stone wall on the Mount of Olives and watching a shepherd leading his sheep. I came to the conclusion that every seminary ought to be equipped with a flock of sheep. Having a future pastor lead sheep around the seminary grounds for a few days may give him some idea of what it means to be a pastor who leads rather than pushes his flock.

Since the Holy Spirit *brings* to us the ministry of our Lord Jesus, we can infer that any leading of the Spirit will be in the form of a pull or a draw rather than a push or a shove. And I believe it is possible for us to discern the difference.

Think of the times in the past when you were tempted by the devil, the world, or your sinful flesh. There was a sense of compulsion. You felt as if you had to do it—now. There is no patience or gentleness with temptation. Occultism, for example, produces obsessive and compulsive behavior. The temptations of the flesh demand immediate gratification. You cannot wait until the next day.

This sense of compulsion, obsession, or immediate gratification is not the manner in which the Holy Spirit leads. He goes before, prepares the way, and gently urges us to follow. If you feel pushed into something, back off. It is probably not the Holy Spirit.

## Anger and Contention

Much of what I talk about on my daily radio talk show deals with apologetics—the defense of the faith against error and deception. I enjoy discussing theology and debating people who hold to different views about the Bible. While I know this is what the Holy Spirit wants me to do, sometimes I don't do it how he wants it done. I become argumentative or contentious.

Some time ago I interviewed a man who had written a book about the end of the world. I did not agree with him. He promoted a theology which, in my opinion, had little if any basis in the clear Word of God. Our discussion ended on a very cordial note, and he thanked me for conducting a good interview.

A week or so later I received a scathing letter from this man. He denounced me as a supercritical person and called me a fool. I was surprised and angry.

So, I sat down at my computer and angrily shot back with a scathing letter of my own.

Well, he responded in kind.

By that time I realized that our interaction was not being led by the Spirit. My attitudes and feelings were not right. We were dealing with each other according to the old sinful nature. I sat down at the computer, looked to the Holy Spirit with prayer and praise, and wrote a kind letter. Later, I got a return letter that was written with the same kindness.

We have to be careful that we do not bite and devour each other with our words, both written and spoken. When we set our minds on the things of the Spirit, we are able to speak the truth and confront error with the proper attitude.

If you ever get into an argument or debate with someone and you sit down at your computer to fire off an angry letter, take time to wait before you mail it. Give yourself a chance to sleep on the matter. Then the next morning, set your mind on the goodness, grace, and mercy of God, and read your letter again. Assess your feelings. If you do not feel at peace about what you said, don't mail your letter.

## There's More to the Process

Using our feelings to discern the leading of the Holy Spirit is only one part of the total process of guidance. I most certainly would not make an important decision based solely on good feelings or a sense of peace. Yet, emotions and feelings do have a part in helping us to make decisions.

Discovering the will of God is a process. We learn to be led by the Spirit as we read the signposts along the way, and discerning our feelings and emotions is one of those signposts.

Being led by the Spirit is a process
to be learned. There are no quick
fixes or simple methods for discerning
the will of God.

# 13

# No Quick Fixes

Supernatural guidance is a very popular subject today. We seem to be living in an age during which many people share a growing anxiety over the realization that their lives, disconnected from any purpose or meaning, are merely drifting aimlessly with no rhyme or reason. To know that a higher power or a spiritual reality exists and is able to give direction provides a source of comfort and connection to something or someone greater than themselves.

There is much available today in the form of "supernatural guidance." Psychic hotlines provide spiritual insight and direction for only $2.99 per minute. *Silva Mind Control* and New Age advocates offer people the opportunity to get their own personal spirit-guide. Betty Eadie's *Embraced by the Light*, a multimillion-copy bestselling book, parts the curtain and provides a glimpse of "heaven" and insights into the meaning and purpose of life from "Jesus" himself. *Ouija* is second only to *Monopoly* in the list of popular board games. Tarot cards, crystal balls, palm reading, and consulting with the dead are popular techniques people use in their attempt to discover some rhyme and reason for their earthly existence.

In the same vein, the subject of guidance or getting to know the will of God is also a popular concern for Christians—if not at times an obsession. Dr. J. I. Packer writes:

> The more earnest and sensitive a believer is, the more likely he or she is to be hung up about guidance. And if I am any judge, the evangelical anxiety level on the subject continues to rise. Why is this? The source of anxiety is that a desire for guidance is linked with uncertainty about how to get it and fear of the consequences of not getting it.[1]

Because we live in a society preoccupied with New Age enlightenment and occult revelations, it is important for us Christians to clearly distinguish the legitimate guidance provided by the Holy Spirit from the counterfeits.

## Process, Not a Quick Fix

I believe that the clearest distinction between occult forms of guidance and the manner in which the Holy Spirit leads is this: Occult techniques offer a quick fix, but the Holy Spirit leads us through a process during which we keep our eyes on the road signs along the way. This process is what Paul is talking about when he says we are to "walk in the Spirit." We walk in a daily relationship with both the Lord Jesus and with our brothers and sisters in Christ, who also have the Holy Spirit.

Christians sometimes use quick-fix techniques to try and find out the will of God. These techniques are not necessarily occultic, but they are unreliable and they can easily lead one astray.

## Fleecing

For example, there is a practice known as "fleecing." We read about it in Judges 6, where Gideon was attempting to discern whether or not God was calling him to lead Israel against the Midianites. One night Gideon put out a fleece and asked God to put dew on the fleece but none on the grass. The Lord obliged. Gideon then asked for the reverse to be true the next night—dew on the grass but none on the fleece. Again, the Lord obliged.

Should we set "fleeces" before God as a means of determining his will for us? For example, "God, if you really want me to marry that man, have him wear a red shirt when we go out tonight." Or, "God, if you are calling me to go to seminary and enter the ministry, have my pastor preach about going into the ministry this next Sunday."

There is no biblical command or basis for "fleecing" God or making "if you will do this, than I will do that" bargains. The book of Acts gives no indication that the apostles sought to know God's will in that manner.

Bargaining with God can have devastating results. Remember the story of Jephthah, who was one of the judges of Israel after Gideon? Before he went to battle with the Ammonites, he made a deal with God:

"If you give the Ammonites into my hands," Jephthah vowed, "whatever comes out of the door of my house to meet me when I return in triumph from the Ammonites will be the LORD's, and I will sacrifice it as a burnt offering" (Judges 11:30-31).

When Jephthah returned home in triumph, it was not a prize animal that came out of his door, but his only child, a daughter, celebrating the victory by dancing to the sound of tambourines. Because he made the vow, he was forced to pay the price. What a tragic story!

A closer look at the story of Gideon reveals it is possible that Gideon was not trying to discover the will of God, but rather, he was trying to get *out* of doing God's will. Gideon knew what God's will was. An angel had visited him and incinerated a sacrifice right before Gideon's eyes by touching it with the tip of his rod. Gideon knew what God wanted; the fleece was his attempt to find a reason not to do it.

Let me illustrate: Suppose on a Saturday night I say, "God, if you want me to go to church tomorrow morning, make it rain so that I can't play golf." If Sunday morning happens to be bright and sunny, I have a reason to blame God for my decision not to go to church and play golf. "After all," I might reason, "he didn't make it rain." That's silliness!

Putting a fleece before God is like seeking guidance by opening your Bible at random and pointing your finger at a verse. The Bible is not a *Ouija* board. There are no quick fixes!

## What About Prayer?

You may have wondered why, in a book about the Holy Spirit's leading in our lives, the subject of prayer has not been discussed. This is not an oversight on my part. There is a reason for it.

It goes without saying that there is great value in prayer, which helps to focus our hearts and minds upon the Lord. Similar to singing hymns and choruses of praise, prayer makes us God-conscious. True prayer arises out of our new life in Christ Jesus.

While God certainly invites us to pray and has promised to hear our prayers, *the Bible does not suggest a cause-and-effect relationship between prayer and being led by the Holy Spirit.*

That may come somewhat as a shock to you. For many Christians, their only venture into the dimension of personal piety is that they pray occasionally. For me to say that the Bible makes no connection between prayer and discerning the will of God or being led by the Spirit might be somewhat surprising, but can you show me one place in the book of Acts where the apostles were led by the Spirit as a direct result of taking the time to pray?

When the Holy Spirit forbade the apostles to enter Asia and Bithynia, the Bible doesn't say that they "prayed about it" and decided that they shouldn't go.

After Paul had seen the vision of the man from Macedonia, why didn't the apostles first "pray about it" before concluding that they should go to Macedonia?

When Paul was told by everyone not to go to Jerusalem, why didn't he first spend the night "praying about it" before he decided to go anyway?

When the apostles decided on how they should receive Gentile converts in the first church convention, prayer was not mentioned (Acts 15).

It shouldn't seem strange that prayer is not mentioned in Acts as a part to the process of seeking God's will. If the apostles *had* sought guidance through prayer, it would have given people the impression that seeking the will of God required, as an answer to prayer, an external, mystical invasion of the mind of the Holy Spirit into the apostlic consciousness. But the lack of prayer confirms the fact that all of the equipment needed to guide and lead the apostles was already within them. Being led by the Spirit is an internal guidance system, not an external, mystical invasion.

Sadly, many Christians today use prayer as a religious exercise that allows them to connect with God. Then after they say, "Amen," they disconnect again and go their own way and do their own thing. The book of Acts assumes that the apostles were living in a constant, conscious relationship with God. They were not going their own way, doing their own thing, and connecting with God only when it came time to make a decision.

## "Did You Pray About It?"

More often than not, when you share your heart with a fellow Christian and explain your dilemma in seeking to discover the will of God in a situation, you will get this question: "Did you pray about it?" That question is exasperating. Sometimes, when asked that question, my sinful nature wants to respond, "No, I felt it was more important to get your advice than to talk to God about it."

Or, if a person is explaining why he or she made a certain decision, he or she will remark, "Well, I prayed about it and decided to do this."

Prayer, however, is not a practice that immediately places everything in our lives into a spiritual context. This type of nonbiblical thinking is often expressed by Christians. You might ask a church member, "How do you know that the decisions you reached in your meeting last night were the will of God?"

Invariably you will get the answer, "Well, we opened the meeting with prayer."

I once heard about a pastor who gathered with his elders to seek the will of God for their church. After they prayed together, they got out the Ouija Board and began to ask it some questions. Did their prayer sanctify the Ouija Board?

It is not my intent to denigrate the practice of prayer. We should keep our communication lines open between ourselves and our God and pray without ceasing (1 Thessalonians 5:17). If we lack wisdom, we should ask the Lord to grant us wisdom, because he gives generously (James 1:5,6). We should seek to be filled with the knowledge of God's will (Colossians 1:9). We should pray for doors of ministry to be opened for us. As Jesus prayed in the Garden of Gethsemane, the words, "Thy will be done" should be in our hearts and on our lips.

What I am trying to say is that prayer is not a substitute for being filled with the Spirit, walking in the Spirit, discerning our thoughts and peace of mind, considering the circumstances, or seeking the counsel of other Christians. Prayer is not a quick fix into finding the will of God. Again, being led by the Spirit is a process, a way of living, not a quick solution, nor an answer to prayer.

It reminds me of the story of the man who was stranded on his housetop as the floodwaters raged around him. He prayed, "Lord, save me!" A rowboat came by and the men on board urged him to get in the boat.

"No thanks," he replied. "The Lord will rescue me."

As the water level got higher, a powerboat came by and the driver begged him to get on board. Again the man on the rooftop responded in the same manner.

As the floodwaters began to engulf him, a helicopter flew over and tossed him a rope.

"Grab the rope! Save yourself!" the men on board pleaded.

"No" he said confidently. "The Lord will save me!"

Finally, the man drowned. As he stood before God, he asked, "Lord, why didn't you save me?"

"I tried," the Lord replied. "I sent you two boats and a helicopter."

The point is simple: Pray, but don't forget to discern what is going on around you.

## Jesus is Not a Spirit Guide

Visualization prayer is a very dangerous practice that is being widely taught among Christians today. It is produced via empty-headed meditation and usually involves journaling. The proponents of this practice get their teachings from the writings of Morton Kelsey, an Episcopalian priest and follower of occult psychiatrist Dr. Carl Jung.

Visualization prayer uses the same occult techniques taught in *Silva Mind Control*. The candidate is encouraged to enter into an altered state of consciousness by developing a passive mind and visualizing the spirit-guide of their choice. Of course, for Christians, that spirit-guide becomes Jesus.

After making "contact" with Jesus, the candidate proceeds to ask him questions and receive his "divine" advice. The dialogue is recorded in a journal, which for some, becomes the "now word of the Lord" or the *rhema* word.

Mark Virkler, in his book *Dialogue with God,* attempts to regurgitate some of Kelsey's occult concepts and make them presentable for unsuspecting evangelicals and charismatics. In regard to getting answers from "Jesus" via the technique of journaling, Virkler writes:

> If you want to, take a pencil and paper and quiet yourself before the Lord. Speak to him what is on your mind. Let him speak back. Then record what he says. If you don't sense a response, ask him a specific question. Relax, and in simple, childlike faith record what seems to be there. You will discover that it is him.[2]

That very much resembles what happens in automatic writing and when you play *Ouija.*

There are some foolish Christians today who operate on the assumption that methodology is neutral. It can be pointed at demons or it can be pointed at the Holy Spirit. This is gross deception. The Bible clearly spells out the methodology for being led by the Holy Spirit. It is a process that involves being filled with the Spirit, renewing our active minds, assessing our emotions and feelings, discerning the circumstances around us, and listening to the advice and counsel that we receive from God's people. You cannot short-circuit the methods of the Holy Spirit by engaging in some occult technique. You may contact a spirit, but it will not be the Holy Spirit.

The Holy Spirit gives ministry, or works of service,

to the people of God. The ministry develops

little by little as the Spirit leads and directs

the "ministers" by knitting them together

in one mind and heart.

# 14

# The Holy Spirit
# and Your Ministry

The end result of being led by the Spirit is effective
ministry or service to God and others. While I believe
the Holy Spirit is willing to lead us in our personal
decision-making, the primary purpose of Spirit-led guidance is to make us more effective members of the Body
of Christ. When the apostle Paul tells us in Romans 12:2
to discover the will of God by testing and examining, he
is speaking in the context of the gifts and ministries
given to God's people. We desire to be led by the Spirit
so that we might fulfill the good works that God has prepared for us to do.

In the book of Acts we can discern some general
principles about how the Holy Spirit called, led, and directed the church and the ministry of the first-century
Christians. Yet what we learn from Scripture about the
life and ministry of the early Christians should not be
codified or turned into doctrinal concepts because the
Holy Spirit works in different ways at different times
with different people. Sometimes Christians make the
mistake of thinking that biblical, historical precedent is

true for all times in all cases. But that's not necessarily true in all matters. There is no precedent in Scripture, for example, of the Holy Spirit leading people into radio, television, or publishing ministries, but obviously he does.

Not all biblical narratives reveal principles that we are supposed to follow today. For example, before the apostles began their ministry, they waited in Jerusalem for ten days, and then when they were gathered together in an upper room the Holy Spirit descended. That, however, does not mean we cannot begin serving the Lord unless we first move to Jerusalem, rent a second-story room, and wait ten days for the Holy Spirit to descend. That would be foolishness.

Of course, if we see a principle in Scripture that is also applicable in the development of effective ministries today, we may want to take note.

Having put in place the basic steps in the process of guidance, let us consider some of the principles by which the Holy Spirit accomplished his work through the believers in the first century.

## Ministry is Entrusted to Individuals

We can observe from Scripture that among the early Christians, ministry was entrusted to individuals. Individuals, of course, make up the Body of Christ, the church. In Colossians 4:17, Paul encourages a certain Archippus to "complete the work you have received in the Lord."

Nowhere in Scripture do we see the Holy Spirit call a particular church into a particular ministry. For example, we know that Paul was a part of the church in Antioch. In Acts 13:1-3, he was sent or ordained into the ministry by the church at Antioch. We know that when he returned from the first missionary journey, he gave a report to the church at Antioch (Acts 14:26-28). But the work he did on his journey ministry was not the ministry of the church at Antioch, but rather, it was his own ministry.

This is an important, practical principle. While I was pastoring a church in Michigan, I began a television ministry. Later, publishing and tape distribution were added. We had a great deal of equipment. After 11 years, I moved to New York. The question arose: What happens to the ministry? Does it remain in Michigan or move with me to New York? The church concluded that the ministry was "my ministry," and not that of the church—even though they had worked with me in developing it. So everything moved to New York with me and the ministry continued from a different location.

The fact that the Holy Spirit entrusts ministries to individuals can be problematic, especially if we come to see the work as "our" ministry and not God's. Competition can arise. Jealousy can be stirred. When we speak of "our ministry," we should not do so with a sense of possessiveness, but rather with a sense of gratitude toward God and the grace with which he has allowed us to serve as his instruments. We are all members of the Body of Christ. What he has is given to one member is for the blessing of all the members. A person who has been led into effective ministry cannot think of himself as being more important than others.

In Romans 12:3-5 Paul wrote:

> By the grace given me I say to every one of you: Do not think of yourself more highly than you ought, but rather think of yourself with sober judgement, in accordance with the measure of faith God has given

you. Just as each of us has one body with many members, and these members do not all have the same function, so in Christ we who are many form one body, and each member belongs to all the others.

I believe it is a clear principle in Scripture that ministry is entrusted to individuals, and individuals, for the sake of accountability, are set into the Body of Christ, the church.

## The Apostolic Team

Even though God entrusted the work of ministry to individuals, the apostles moved together as a team, each relying upon the other for help and guidance. For example, Paul was willing to take other men along with him to share in the work. Decisions were group decisions.

By recognizing that God gave ministries to individuals, the apostles were able to solve certain problems. For example, when Paul and Barnabas did not agree over whether or not to take John Mark with them on their second missionary journey (Acts 15:36-41), they decided to split up. Since they could not agree on what God's will was, they concluded that they should each go their separate way and fulfill the ministry that had been given to each of them. There is nothing in Scripture that indicates that either Paul or Barnabas was wrong in not being willing to submit to the other's direction. Nor did the church at Antioch, of which they were members, choose to settle the issue.

As a result, the ministry was multiplied. Barnabas, who had been given a ministry by the Holy Spirit and commissioned by the church at Antioch, wanted to share that ministry with John Mark. He did, and sailed for Cyprus. Paul, on the other hand, who also had been given a ministry and was also sent out by the church, did not want to share his ministry with Mark because he felt Mark was too young and not dependable. So, he invited Silas to share in his ministry, and together they went thought Syria and Cilicia.

When Paul and Silas arrived at Lystra, where Timothy lived, Paul decided to share the ministry with him as well and take him along on the journey. Paul had Timothy circumcised so as not to offend the Jews, and, probably within a few days, the journey commenced. The story continues in Acts 16:6-10:

> Paul and his companions traveled throughout the region of Phrygia and Galatia, having been kept by the Holy Spirit from preaching the word in the province of Asia. When they came to the border of Mysia, they tried to enter Bithynia, but the Spirit of Jesus would not allow them to. So they passed by Mysia and went down to Troas. During the night, Paul had a vision of a man of Macedonia standing and begging him, "Come over to Macedonia and help us." After Paul had seen the vision, we got ready at once to leave for Macedonia, concluding that God had called us to preach the gospel to them.

There are a number of interesting observations we can make from those verses.

As we learned in an earlier chapter, the Holy Spirit hindered them from going into Asia and Bithynia—perhaps by giving them negative impressions or circumstances. So they went down to Troas, a city on the Aegean Sea opposite Europe or Macedonia.

At Troas, we know that Luke was invited to join the apostolic team. How do we know? If you look at Acts

16:6-10, you will notice that the preposition changes from "they" to "we." Since Luke is the author of the book of Acts, the "we" had to be a reference that included himself. We therefore know that he lived in Troas and accompanied Paul, Silas, and Timothy when they left Troas. On their way home, the preposition changes back to "they" immediately after they depart from Troas.

While at Troas, Paul had a vision or dream. He saw a man from Europe or Macedonia urging him to cross the Aegean and begin missionary work in Europe. *But was the vision from the Holy Spirit?* There are other sources for dreams and visions. It might have emerged from his subconscious. He could have had a fever or an upset stomach the night before. It might have been the devil. How was Paul to know?

It was for this very reason that he shared his ministry with others. He needed them.

## Knit Together

The Bible says that the apostles concluded that Paul's vision was from the Holy Spirit (Acts 16:10). What does that mean? The KJV says that the apostles "assuredly gathered" that the Lord was leading them to Europe. What does the Greek say?

The Greek word *sumbibazo,* which is translated "concluding" actually means "to be knit together." It is the same word used in Ephesians 4:16 and Colossians 2:19; it describes the church as being "held together" or "knit together." The apostolic team was "knit together" in their decision to go to Europe. I wonder how they were knit together?

We do not know what caused them to agree on the direction, but, based on some of what we have already learned about being led by the Spirit, we can surmise that there might have been certain factors involved in their decision.

Perhaps Luke, who lived in Troas, had on another occasion gotten the impression or idea that the Gospel should be preached on the other side of the Aegean Sea in Europe.

Perhaps Silas felt very much at peace about Paul's vision. He had already encountered two situations—at the Asian border and right outside Bithynia, when the Holy Spirit forbade them to go any further. But this time, he probably felt a sense of peace. After hearing about Paul's vision, he may have said, "That's it! I feel good about this!"

Perhaps Timothy had encountered some circumstances that seemed to be opening the door to go Europe.

What we do know for sure is that all four men agreed that Paul's vision was the Holy Spirit telling them to go to Europe, and they immediately got moving. So while the ministry was entrusted to Paul, the decision to go was made as a group.

## The Value of Consensus

There are churches and ministries today that make group decisions on the basis of consensus. If there is no consensus—even if only one person happens to disagree—the decision is tabled until a time when a consensus is able to be reached. This practice is based on the premise that the Holy Spirit would not tell one person one thing and another person something different. Much like the apostles, such ministry teams move on the basis of being "knit together."

When a group functions in this way, the responsibility for the decision is able to be shared with all the participants. Sharing responsibility is important and beneficial, as we can see from the circumstances that resulted from the apostles' joint decision.

During their visit in Philippi, Paul and Silas were thrown into prison after Paul had cast a demon out of a young slave girl. How did they respond to this seeming setback? Acts 16:25 says that they sang praises to God in the midst of the horrible prison surroundings.

Since they were both responsible for the decision, and they both believed it was the will of God, neither could complain about their circumstances. And of course, after the earthquake opened the prison gates, they knew with certainty that it was the will of God for them to be there.

If you had a vision for beginning a certain ministry in your church or community and that ministry now includes a number of other people, you'll want to share decision-making with the others who are involved. Because you started the ministry, you may find yourself wanting to make all the decisions, but that will not further the growth of the ministry. Share the ministry! New ideas as to how to enlarge, develop, and increase the ministry's effectiveness will probably come from the other participants. Share responsibility for decision-making. If you don't and the ministry fails, you will get all the blame and rightfully so!

## Little by Little

Jesus told his disciples that they would be his witnesses in Jerusalem, in all Judea and Samaria, and to the ends of the earth (Acts 1:8).

Notice that the disciples' ministry was to develop little by little. The church was first established and set in order in Jerusalem. In Acts 8, they extended their outreach to Samaria. In Acts 10, the Gentiles were brought in. In Acts 13, the missionary journeys began. On this basis, we might establish a principle of concentric circles. Before going to the ends of the earth, the Holy Spirit desires to establish the ministry locally.

We might compare this principle with the manner in which Joshua was led to take the land of Israel. The principle was "little by little" (Deuteronomy 7:22). In Exodus 23:30, the Lord told the people of Israel, "Little by little I will drive them out before you, until you have *increased enough* to take possession of the land" (emphasis added).

If you have a vision or an idea to begin a ministry and you believe it is from the Holy Spirit, then start by establishing the ministry in your own backyard. As your ministry grows, you can gradually extend its sphere of influence. I believe that is a sound principle defining the way the Holy Spirit works in leading his people.

## Church Ministries

In most denominations, various ministries are established, developed, and conducted by the denomination's head office in behalf of the local churches. While the churches conduct their local ministry, the denomination's head office oversees the outreach ministries, which may include radio, television, publishing, world missions, social concerns, and the like.

Denominational structures are neither strange nor wrong. The institution, receiving support from the affiliated churches and having a variety of resources and manpower at their disposal, should be able to accomplish far more than the local churches or individuals would be able to do on their own.

The problem is, it's difficult to apply some of the principles we've gleaned from the book of Acts to the ministries conducted by denominations. I do not say this to criticize the ministries of denominational groups. The radio program I host is a denominational ministry that has been effective, but still, there are inherent problems when denominations run ministries.

We should not be surprised that most of the effective ministries in evangelism, radio and television, publishing, youth ministries, and social ministries are independent operations not connected to or sponsored by a specific denomination. Television preachers such as James Kennedy, Jerry Falwell, and Pat Robertson are all members of specific denominations, yet their television outreach is operated independently of their denominations and exceeds anything produced by their denominations.

If you were to study the development of many of the large independent ministries such as Pat Robertson's CBN, or Charles Colson's Prison Fellowship, or Loren Cunningham's Youth with a Mission, or Bill Bright's Campus Crusade for Christ, I would not at all be surprised if you discovered that they used most of the principles of guidance that I have been sharing with you.

Each of these ministries probably began when the Holy Spirit implanted an idea in the mind of an individual. The Spirit prepared the way and set the stage. The individual who got the idea shared the ministry with others, who became knit together in a common goal and purpose. As a result, the ministry began to grow little by little.

As I said previously, the operation of the Holy Spirit in developing and increasing a ministry is not limited to the way he did things in the first century. The principles we glean from the book of Acts are not necessarily normative for every place and every time. Yet, *if we discover that ministries that are in line with these principles are more effective than ministries that are not, we may want to give these principles careful consideration.*

Within denomonational ministries there is usually no recognition that ministry is entrusted to individuals. Any ministry becomes a "ministry of the church" rather than the ministry of a visionary individual within the church. The reason for that is not difficult to understand; denominational structures exist to promote the denomination, not the individuals within it.

Since most denominational structures are organized around a corporate model, decisions are not the result of hearts being knit together, but are rather handed down through the corporate ladder. The dynamic sense of the Holy Spirit leading and directing the ministry is often replaced with a well-oiled bureaucratic machinery.

Given the phenomenal rise of independent ministries over the past 25 years coupled with the decline experienced by many of the mainline denominations, the powers that be within institutional organizations should be taking a long, hard look at the manner in which they function. Perhaps there is a better way for them to carry on the work of ministry.

## One Last Step

All of our principles are now in place, and all that is left is for you to put into practice what you have learned. How do you do that? Do you wait for the Lord to make his will clear to you, or do you step out? That's what we're going to talk about next.

The Holy Spirit directs our path

as we step out in faith.

Even if we are wrong, God does not reject us.

Seeking to be led by the Holy Spirit produces

an exciting, dynamic lifestyle.

# 15

# Get Moving!

In the third chapter of Joshua we read the story about the children of Israel crossing the Jordan and entering into the promised land. They were charting new territory; they had never been there before.

The Lord God instructed Joshua to have the priests, bearing the Ark of the Covenant, go before the people. When the priests reached the edge of the Jordan, which was at flood stage, they were to "get their feet wet." They had to walk carefully—bearing the precious Ark of the Covenant—into the swollen, probably rapidly flowing river. As their feet hit the water, the river parted before them.

I am sure the priests would have preferred to have the river part *before* they entered into the water, but that was not the way God planned it. They had to step into the water before it parted. Today the Holy Spirit expects us to do the same—to step out, be active, seek his will, knock on some doors, and take responsibility. I like the way Blaine Smith puts it:

> I would like to suggest that there is truth in the adage: *God can't steer a parked car.* In many cases, God waits until he sees us taking responsibility

before he brings the right opportunity along, even though that opportunity might not be directly related to our personal efforts.[1]

## Waiting on God

A number of years ago a small, charismatic, discipleship-type fellowship moved into the small town in Michigan where I was the pastor of church. Their "pastor," a young man who had been "ordained" in an independent fellowship in Texas, had no theological training. He was a nice man and rather intelligent. Most of the participants in the fellowship were college graduates.

The group, which comprised about four families, bought a farm and set up mobile homes on the property. Their intention was to make a living on the farm, while "waiting on God" to lead them into some kind of ministry in our area.

They knew that my church was deeply involved in spiritual renewal. Their pastor often attended our Sunday night prayer and praise meeting. He knew that we had various ministries involving books, tapes, music, and so on.

One Sunday evening, after our prayer and praise gathering was over, he approached me. After some small talk, he said, "I hate to say this brother, but I must speak. I believe that what you are doing here is 'in the flesh.' God does not build his church with human might or power, but by his Spirit. You should be waiting on God to act."

I was somewhat taken back by his statement. We decided to get together that week to talk more, and we did.

In the course of our discussion, it became clear that we disagreed over the role of the human will and mind in seeking to do God's will. He believed that man's will and intellect were corrupt and could not be used. God had to initiate the work by his Spirit. According to my viewpoint, man's will and intellect had been corrupted by sin but had been redeemed. I concluded our discussion by saying, "The Holy Spirit expects us to exercise our will, engage our thinking, and step out in faith."

He did not agree.

To make a long story short, eventually the fellowship went broke. They did not know anything about farming. Their crops failed. Disillusioned by their failure, they disbanded and left the community. They never did anything except sit and wait for God to act, and apparently he didn't.

There are people who never accomplish anything because they never try. They are not willing to step out, test the water, and see what possibilities lie ahead.

## A Frightening Experience

Sometimes stepping out in faith can be a frightening experience. I got to a point about 20 years ago where I had to make a decision one way or the other. The "Bread of Life" ministry had developed to the place where it demanded much of my time. I was also frequently on the road. The problem was, I was still the pastor of a church that also required a great deal of my attention. As a result of my outside involvement, the church was suffering. Something had to be done. I either had to shut down the outside ministry or develop it full-time.

After receiving the advice and counsel of many other people and carefully discerning the circumstances, I decided to *step out in faith* into the "Bread of Life" ministry. So the church brought in another pastor who would receive my salary, and I made plans to earn my living from the ministry, which, at that time, was bringing in some resources, but not a sufficient amount to support me, my wife, and four children. Since the other pastor owned a home in the area, the church allowed me to keep my free housing in the parsonage. I also continued to serve the church on a limited basis but without any salary.

Because "Bread of Life" did not bring sufficient income, I needed to find some ways to get additional support. So, in order to establish my salary, I set up some situations for myself. One man told me that he had some stock that he would sell; he planned to use the proceeds from the sale to help support me. As he put it, "I'll put some feet under your vision." Another man, who was a part of my church, told me that he would commit a certain amount each month for my support. A small prayer group in a neighboring city told me that they would gather an offering each week that would go to me. When I sat down and added up all the figures, it appeared that I was all set. The other pastor came in, and my monthly salary ended.

Within two weeks, I received some bad news. The man who owned the stock sold it, but found out it was worthless. The second man was investigated by the IRS and came up wanting. And one member of the prayer group in the neighboring city lost his job, and the other members decided to support him instead of me. I was stuck!

That's when I realized that although I was claiming to step out in faith and trust the Lord to provide for me and my family, I was also trying to improve the situation through my own efforts to find additional support. After I heard all the bad news, a funny thought hit me:

*Now what are you going? The only alternative you have left is to trust God.* But being put into a situation in which God is your only hope is not a bad situation to be in.

God is good! The Lord began providing for us immediately. The phone started ringing, and I received numerous opportunities to do seminars, conferences, and retreats. We were able to purchase a trailer and spent our summers on the road. It was incredible. We lived that way for three years before moving to New York. In fact, we fared better financially for those three years than in any other three-year period during which I received a salary.

If you are faced with a decision that involves your family's financial security, you must move very carefully. Please keep in mind that I was faced with a decision that involved little risk. First, I was not contemplating giving up my salary in order to begin a ministry. The ministry was already there and merely needed more attention. And second, I still had an entire congregation of supportive people around me. The possibility did not exist that I would go broke and we would end up homeless.

## Don't Be Afraid to Be Wrong

When we attempt to discern the will of God, we will have times when we make mistakes. God knows that will happen because we only have childish, partial knowledge (*see* 1 Corinthians 13:12). I would much rather seek the will of God, set my mind on the Spirit, discern my thoughts and impressions, look for circumstances, assess my feelings, seek the advice of other Christians, and make a decision and perhaps be wrong instead of relying upon my own unaided reasoning and common sense and be wrong. I would rather at least seek to be led by the Holy Spirit—and according to the Bible, this is what God wants me to do.

During my 30 years in the ministry, I have knocked on many doors. Some have opened while others have remained shut. I have pursued opportunities. When someone suggests an idea to me, I take it seriously. It may be the Holy Spirit.

There have also been occasions when I have knocked on doors and have been embarrassed by the response. Some of the people who have seen that happen to me may think I'm a bit strange. But to tell you the truth, I don't care what other people think. If you don't step out and seek opportunities for ministry, you will not accomplish a great deal. You have to get your feet wet before the river will part.

Then, of course, there are those incredibly exciting times when you pursue what you believe to be the direction of the Holy Spirit and everything falls into place. Circumstances come together. "By chance" you meet people who share the same vision you do. Resources become readily available, and an exciting ministry develops.

## My Challenge to You

If you are a Christian, the person of the Holy Spirit dwells in you. He has a will for you. He has prepared a ministry for you. He can lead and guide you. He wants to use you. Are you available?

Put into practice what I have shared with you. I am not asking you to adopt a new theology or discard any doctrines, but to simply recognize the reality of the person of the Holy Spirit. If you learn to distinguish the

Spirit-inspired ideas from your flesh-inspired ones and use God's Word and worship to help you be filled with his Spirit, you will sense a new mind within you. When you get ideas that you believe are Spirit-led, follow them. See what happens! And don't be afraid to get involved with the visions and ministries of others.

There are many faithful Christians who sit in church Sunday after Sunday without truly becoming involved. Maybe you are one of them. You support the work of the church, you believe in Jesus, and you are heaven-bound, but perhaps you have never really been involved in any type of ministry. I challenge you to change that! You are a part of the body of Christ. You have been given gifts for Christian service. God has prepared good works for you to walk in. Step out! And see what God has prepared for you.

# Appendix

# The Ministry of the Holy Spirit

There is widespread disagreement and contention in the church today about the work of the Holy Spirit. What charismatics claim is the reviving work of the Holy Spirits is defined by other Christians as deception. The advent of psychological techniques has prompted discussion over the nature and source of the fruit of Spirit. The revival of ancient mysticism and the growing popularity of New Age has introduced eastern spirituality into the church. We are living in an age in which a clear definition of the Holy Spirit's work is vitally important so we can avoid deception.

While it is not possible to present a thorough treatment of the Spirit's work in a brief appendix, let us briefly consider four specific biblical truths concerning the Holy Spirit's ministry and the practical implications of those truths for us today.

## A. *The Ministry of the Holy Spirit Extends the Ministry of Jesus Christ*

In the death and resurrection of our Lord Jesus Christ, God the Father accomplished all that was necessary for life and salvation. There is nothing more that God needs to do to save, redeem, or justify sinful mankind. God, for example, does not have a plan to save America. He already completed his plan at Calvary. When Jesus said, "It is finished" (John 19:30), he did not mean, "To be continued."

The apostle Paul makes clear in his letter to the Colossians that all spiritual blessings are found in Christ Jesus (Colossians 1:19,20; 2:3,9,10). But the question remains: How do all the blessings of life and salvation accomplished for us in Christ Jesus nearly 2,000 years ago come to us today?

Through the work of the Holy Spirit.

Jesus told his disciples, "It is for your good that I am going away. Unless I go away, the Counselor will not come to you; but if I go, I will send him to you" (John 16:7).

In Acts 1:1,2, Luke spoke of his Gospel as the beginning of Jesus' ministry. After Jesus ascended into heaven, Luke said that Jesus continued to give instructions to his apostles through the Holy Spirit.

On the Day of Pentecost, when the Holy Spirit became the permanent resident within the church, Jesus Christ returned to his disciples. *The ministry of the Holy Spirit is the continuation and extension of the Ministry of Jesus Christ.* The apostles, when they described the work of santification, readily interchanged the person of the Holy Spirit with the person of Jesus Christ. For example, being led by the Holy Spirit is the same as being led by the Spirit of Jesus (Acts 16:6,7); being controlled by the Holy Spirit means being controlled by the Spirit of Christ (Romans 8:9); living in the Spirit means living in Christ; walking in the Spirit means walking in Christ (Colossians 2:6); and being filled with the Spirit means being filled with the presence of Christ. The Holy Spirit cannot be separated from Jesus Christ.

*Implications:*

1.   If the Holy Spirit had not come, we would be dependent upon special appearances of the risen Christ so that
we might believe in him and learn of him. The Bible
teachers and evangelists to whom Jesus appeared would
be considered the apostles and prophets of our age. The
problem is, Jesus never promised that he would continue
to make appearances after he ascended into heaven.
Instead, his ministry is extended through the ministry of
the Holy Spirit. The apostle Paul, when he spoke about
meeting the Lord Jesus on the road to Damascus, spoke
of himself as one "born out of due time" (1Corinthians
15:8 KJV). In other words, the meeting happened beyond
the age when Jesus made postresurrection appearances.
Of course, it goes without saying that Jesus Christ is not
a "spirit guide." Nor did he ever promise, as some people
teach, to send his mother to us to reveal hidden truth.

On the basis of Jesus' words and promises, we must
conclude that claims to such appearances for the sake
of providing people with wisdom and guidance are
fraudulent. We do not need to seek discernment about
whether Jesus or Mary appeared at a certain time and
place. When Scripture is clear, there is no discernment
needed. The only promise that Jesus made was that the
Holy Spirit would come and lead us into all the truth.

People who claim that Jesus appeared to them and
revealed specific truths are attempting to entice you to
accept the authority and credibility of their words. Do
not be deceived!

2.   Since the Holy Spirit continues the ministry of
Jesus Christ, to seek discernment by asking the question,
"What would Jesus do?" in a given situation is very rele-
vant. For example, would Jesus blow up at people and
knock them over? Would he poke people in the stomach

and cause them to laugh? Would he throw his power across the room and knock over three rows of people? Would he cause his disciples to be "slain in the Spirit" and have "carpet time"?

If we believe that specific antics and practices are not consistent with Christ's ministry as revealed in the four Gospels, we could readily conclude that they are either fraudulent, psychologically induced, psychic, or occultic. The Spirit's ministry is an extension of Jesus' ministry; it is not "another" or a different ministry.

## B. *The Holy Spirit Glorifies Jesus*

Jesus defined what the Holy Spirit would do and how he would be identified. He said that the Holy Spirit would "take from what is mine and show it to you." The Holy Spirit would not speak about nor glorify himself, but would speak about and glorify the risen, ascended Son of God (John 16:12-15).

The ministry of the Holy Spirit is to glorify the Lord Jesus and deliver to us the blessings of life and salvation that were won at Calvary.

### Implications
1.   The Holy spirit will not draw attention to himself. You will not find the Holy Spirit where the focus is upon the Holy Spirit. Rather, you will find the Spirit where the gospel of Jesus Christ is proclaimed in its truth and purity—where Jesus is worshiped as King over kings, and Lord over lords.

The Holy Spirit does not glorify himself. I do not believe that he will lead me to say, "Good morning, Holy Spirit," as the title of one popular book suggests. I believe he will lead me to reverently pray, "Good morning, Lord Jesus."

2.  Since the Spirit's purpose is to bring us to faith in Jesus Christ so that we might receive the blessings of life and salvation, there are no Holy Spirit-produced manifestations, fruit, or life-changing dynamics where there is no faith relationship with Jesus Christ. It is possible for psychological methods, mystical techniques, and the sociological dynamics of group pressure to produce life-changing dynamics for all people regardless of their relationship with Jesus Christ, but these are not the work of the Holy Spirit.

When we assess movements that offer positive, life-changing results such as Alcoholics Anonymous, Marriage Encounter, or even Promise Keepers, we must carefully identify the dynamic that is involved. If the dynamic produces positive results for all participants regardless of their faith in Jesus Christ, then it is not the fruit of the Holy Spirit. I'm not saying that to condemn certain movements. I'm just pointing out that participation may be beneficial to us, but it's possible that the results are being produced by natural causes.

I knew a woman who worked in a counseling center at a large university. She interacted with numerous psychologists. One day she told me, "I work with some of the kindest, most loving men and women I have ever met, but most of them are atheists."

## C. The Holy Spirit Works Through the Word of God

How does the Holy Spirit bring to us the blessings of life and salvation that are "in Christ Jesus"? Does he operate directly upon the hearts and minds of people where and when he chooses, or does he need a vehicle through which he works?

The issue of whether or not the Holy Spirit required a vehicle was the source of much debate at the time of the Reformation. Both Luther and Calvin, responding to the claims of the mystics, enthusiasts, and "heavenly prophets," affirmed the clear biblical position that the Holy Spirit operates through the means of the Word of God.

In Romans 1:16, the apostle Paul speaks of the preaching of the gospel as "the power of God for the salvation of everyone who believes."

In Romans 10:6-17, Paul directs his hearers to the Word of God as the means whereby Jesus comes and creates faith. Faith comes by hearing the Word of God.

In 1 Corinthians 1:21-24, Paul affirms the truth that God has chosen to save the world by the foolishness of preaching the gospel of Jesus Christ.

In Ephesians 5:18-19, the experience of being filled with the Spirit is connected to the practice of singing hymns, psalms, and spiritual songs. (For a full treatment of this subject, review chapter 7 in this book.)

Throughout Scripture, the Holy Spirit is connected to the Word of God. While the Holy Spirit is our only teacher and he will lead us into all the truth, the Bible is his only textbook.

*Implications:*

1.   The Holy Spirit is present in the midst of his people where the Word of God is being taught and proclaimed. Some popular preachers claim to "release" the Spirit or call down the Spirit into an assembly. In some situations, a distinction seems to be made between the preaching of the Word of God and the ministry of the Holy Spirit. It is almost as if, after the sermon is over, "showtime" begins.

However, the Holy Spirit is *not* released via human agency. We receive the Holy Spirit from Jesus Christ; he comes to us through the Word of God. There are no human dispensers of the Holy Spirit or "Holy Ghost Bartenders." Those who claim such titles are guilty of arrogance and presumption.

2.   There is nothing in the New Testament to suggest that the power of the Holy Spirit connected to the Word of God is more effective in some ages than in other ages. Nor is the desire of the Holy Spirit to bring people to salvation greater in times of revival and reformation than it is under more normal circumstances. This is a common misconception today among those who believe that revival comes as the result of praying for a fresh outpouring of the Holy Spirit.

Throughout history there have been times of revival, of reformation, and of spiritual awakening, but these were not caused by a fresh outpouring or new wave of the Holy Spirit. It would be very wrong to suggest that there are people who ended up in hell because the Holy Spirit chose not to have a revival during the age in which they lived. If the Holy Spirit works through the Word of God and God's Word remains constant in every generation, the cause of revivals and awakenings would have to be sought in other variables.

In nineteenth-century, post-enlightenment Germany, a pastor by the name of August Tholuck said, "If per-chance a hawker of indulgences were to appear among us, he would not do a good business; for nobody has a disqui-eted and alarmed conscience."

In the sixteenth century, as a prelude to the Refor-mation, the people of Germany had conscience problems. They were concerned with the issue of sin. When the

Roman Catholic Church offered indulgences for sale, it became a good business. But the conditions were also ripe for the preaching of the gospel of Jesus Christ. So when Luther discovered the great truth of justification by grace through faith because of Christ and he clearly proclaimed the same, great reformation and revival occurred.

For revival to occur in our age, the preaching of the law, judgment, and wrath of God is necessary so that the hearts of people are prepared to hear the Gospel. If we choose to downplay human sin because it is not a politically correct subject, emphasize self-esteem, and seek to promote morality without relationship with Jesus Christ, then we dare not complain about the lack of revival.

Rather than looking heavenward and expecting God to bring revival, let us be about the business that God has given us—namely, the preaching of the whole counsel of God. Praying for revival in our nation means praying that God would use the preaching of his law as the instrument to break our human pride and bring us to repentance so that out of a guilty conscience we kneel before the cross of Jesus Christ. Before such revival can be extended to the nations, it must begin with the church. A feel-good Christianity coupled with moralizing sermons and self-aggrandizing spirituality is a monumental hindrance to revival.

## D. The Holy Spirit and the Will of the Christian

Since the Bible defines unbelievers as being dead in their trespasses and sin (Ephesians 2:1,5; Colossians 2:13), there is nothing they can do by way of human reason or strength to be saved. Spiritually dead people cannot make spiritual decisions. It is the Holy Spirit, working through the preaching of the gospel, who brings the unbeliever to faith (Ephesians 2:8,9). Theologically, this is called justification.

In justification, the Holy Spirit acts upon the heart and will of the unbeliever externally. He operates through the Word of God, which speaks to the human condition

After conversion, the person (now a Christian) is enabled to cooperate with the work of the Holy Spirit in sanctification. In this work, Paul called Christians to continually be active. They should think differently by setting their minds on the things of the Spirit (Romans 8:5-8). They should deliver the works of their old sinful nature over to death and walk in the Spirit (Galatians 5:16-25). They should sing spiritual songs and put the Word of Christ in their hearts (Colossians 3:16).

In sanctification, the work of the Holy Spirit is internal. While he still works through the Word of God that has been recieved into the heart, he sanctifies, leads, and guides the Christian via an internal operation, working upon the mind, the will, and the emotions.

*Implications:*

There are many churches today that have a rich and dynamic understanding of justification but are weak in teaching sanctification. While they are quick to point out that there is nothing a person can do to be saved, they fail to teach Christians how to live and walk in the Spirit once they are saved. Very often, sanctification becomes nothing more than a list of moral directives.

A clear distinction must be made between the work of the Holy Spirit in justification and the work of the Holy Spirit in sanctification.